T0193731

Genesis
God Cares

Genesis
God Cares

A Commentary

Sirak James

WestBow
PRESS®
A DIVISION OF THOMAS NELSON
& ZONDERVAN

WestBow Press books may be ordered through booksellers or by contacting:

WestBow Press
A Division of Thomas Nelson & Zondervan
1663 Liberty Drive
Bloomington, IN 47403
www.westbowpress.com
1 (866) 928-1240

ISBN: 978-1-9736-3403-4 (sc)
ISBN: 978-1-9736-3402-7 (e)

Library of Congress Control Number: 2018908287

Print information available on the last page.

WestBow Press rev. date: 07/16/2018

To the reader:

In order for this book to produce its desired effect, it should be read together with a Bible; for English, the King James Version is most effective. It should also be pointed out that this book was written in chiastic form. The center of the chiasm is the word "Joseph's" in the middle of chapter thirty-seven, in the sentence, "God's plan for Joseph's life began unfolding." May God richly bless you as you take this journey together with Him.

He hath made everything beautiful in His time: also He hath set the world in their heart, so that no man can find out the work that God maketh from the beginning to the end. – *Ecclesiastes 3:11*

Chapter 1

In the beginning God created the heaven and the earth. And the earth was without form, and void; and darkness was upon the face of the deep. And the Spirit of God moved upon the face of the waters.

God's presence could be felt on the earth from the very beginning of time.

And God said, Let there be light: and there was light. And God saw the light, that it was good: and God divided the light from the darkness. And God called the light Day, and the darkness He called Night. And the evening and the morning were the first day.

God's first act of creation provided Him with a means to see the rest of His work.

And God said, Let there be a firmament in the midst of the waters, and let it divide the waters from the waters. And God made the firmament, and divided the waters which were under the firmament from the waters which were above the firmament: and it was so. And God called the firmament Heaven. And the evening and the morning were the second day.

God organized the space above ground.

And God said, Let the waters under the heaven be gathered together unto one place, and let the dry land appear: and it was so. And God called the dry land

Earth; and the gathering together of the waters called He Seas: and God saw that it was good.

God continued organizing, this time on the surface of the earth itself.

And God said, Let the earth bring forth grass, the herb yielding seed, and the fruit tree yielding fruit after his kind, whose seed is in itself, upon the earth: and it was so. And the earth brought forth grass, and herb yielding seed after his kind, and the tree yielding fruit, whose seed was in itself, after his kind: and God saw that it was good. And the evening and the morning were the third day.

The first life, plant life, would give life to all other life on the earth.

And God said, Let there be lights in the firmament of the heaven to divide the day from the night; and let them be for signs, and for seasons, and for days, and years: and let them be for lights in the firmament of the heaven to give light upon the earth: and it was so. And God made two great lights; the greater light to rule the day, and the lesser light to rule the night: He made the stars also. And God set them in the firmament of the heaven to give light upon the earth, and to rule over the day and over the night, and to divide the light from the darkness: and God saw that it was good. And the evening and the morning were the fourth day.

The celestial bodies were given to guide us by giving light and direction and to provide a way for us to tell the time.

And God said, Let the waters bring forth abundantly the moving creature that hath life, and fowl that may fly above the earth in the open firmament of heaven. And God created great whales, and every living creature that moveth, which the

waters brought forth abundantly, after their kind, and every winged fowl after his kind: and God saw that it was good. And God blessed them, saying, Be fruitful, and multiply, and fill the waters in the seas, and let fowl multiply in the earth. And the evening and the morning were the fifth day.

The first living creatures were to fill the earth and the seas, and they were to bring joy to all who beheld them.

And God said, Let the earth bring forth the living creature after his kind, cattle, and creeping thing, and beast of the earth after his kind: and it was so. And God made the beast of the earth after his kind, and cattle after their kind, and every thing that creepeth upon the earth after his kind: and God saw that it was good.

These creatures were created just under humankind and were magnificent to look upon.

And God said, Let Us make man in Our image, after Our likeness: and let them have dominion over the fish of the sea, and over the fowl of the air, and over the cattle, and over all the earth, and over every creeping thing that creepeth upon the earth. So God created man in His own image, in the image of God created He him; male and female created He them. And God blessed them, and God said unto them, Be fruitful, and multiply, and replenish the earth, and subdue it: and have dominion over the fish of the sea, and over the fowl of the air, and over every living thing that moveth upon the earth.

The first man and woman and their descendants were to rule with goodness over the entire creation.

And God said, Behold, I have given you every herb bearing seed, which is upon the face of all the earth, and every tree, in the which is the fruit of a tree yielding seed; to you it shall be for meat.

The original diet of the human race was fruit.

And to every beast of the earth, and to every fowl of the air, and to every thing that creepeth upon the earth, wherein there is life, I have given every green herb for meat: and it was so.

The rest of creation would live off other plant life.

And God saw every thing that He had made, and behold, it was very good. And the evening and the morning were the sixth day.

God was happy with His work.

Chapter 2

Thus the heavens and the earth were finished, and all the host of them. And on the seventh day God ended His work which He had made; and He rested on the seventh day from all His work which He had made. And God blessed the seventh day, and sanctified it: because that in it He had rested from all His work which God created and made.

God established the seventh day as an eternal memorial of what He gave to us during the week of creation.

These are the generations of the heavens and of the earth when they were created, in the day that the LORD God made the earth and the heavens, and every plant of the field before it was in the earth, and every herb of the field before it grew: for the LORD God had not caused it to rain upon the earth, and there was not a man to till the ground. But there went up a mist from the earth, and watered the whole face of the ground.

This utopia needed no human effort to maintain.

And the LORD God formed man of the dust of the ground, and breathed into his nostrils the breath of life; and man became a living soul.

God carved by hand this first man from the ground, and He personally breathed life into the man's body.

And the LORD God planted a garden eastward in Eden; and there He put the man whom He had formed. And out of the ground made the LORD God to grow every tree that is pleasant to the sight, and good for food; the tree of life also in the midst of the garden, and the tree of knowledge of good and evil.

God prepared for the first man a special home that was beautiful and that would sustain him forever.

And a river went out of Eden to water the garden; and from thence it was parted, and became into four heads. The name of the first is Pison: that is it which compasseth the whole land of Havilah, where there is gold; and the gold of that land is good: there is bdellium and the onyx stone. And the name of the second river is Gihon: the same is it that compasseth the whole land of Ethiopia. And

the name of the third river is Hiddekel: that is it which goeth toward the east of Assyria. And the fourth river is Euphrates.

These four rivers continued to other paradise-like places.

And the LORD God took the man, and put him into the garden of Eden to dress it and to keep it. And the LORD God commanded the man, saying, Of every tree of the garden thou mayest freely eat: but of the tree of the knowledge of good and evil, thou shalt not eat of it: for in the day that thou eatest thereof thou shalt surely die.

Eating from this forbidden tree would cause the man to sever his connection with God.

And the LORD God said, It is not good that the man should be alone; I will make him an help meet for him.

God did not want the first human being to feel lonely.

And out of the ground the LORD God formed every beast of the field, and every fowl of the air; and brought them unto Adam to see what he would call them: and whatsoever Adam called every living creature, that was the name thereof.

Adam personally knew every creature on the earth.

And Adam gave names to all cattle, and to the fowl of the air, and to every beast of the field; but for Adam there was not found an help meet for him.

None of these creatures were equal to him in intellect.

And the LORD God caused a deep sleep to fall upon Adam, and he slept: and He took one of his ribs, and closed up the flesh instead thereof; and the rib, which

the LORD God had taken from man, made He a woman, and brought her unto the man. And Adam said, This is now bone of my bones, and flesh of my flesh: she shall be called woman, because she was taken out of man.

The first woman was incredibly beautiful, and she was created as an equal to Adam in every way.

Therefore shall a man leave his father and his mother, and shall cleave unto his wife: and they shall be one flesh. And they were both naked, the man and his wife, and were not ashamed.

The original plan for the marriage relationship between a man and woman was for it to be one of intimacy and trust.

Chapter 3

Now the serpent was more subtle than any beast of the field which the LORD God had made. And he said unto the woman, Yea, hath God said, Ye shall not eat of every tree of the garden?

The serpent wanted to trick the woman into eating fruit from the Tree of Knowledge of Good and Evil before he did.

And the woman said unto the serpent, We may eat of the fruit of the trees of the garden: but of the fruit of the tree which is in the midst of the garden, God hath said, Ye shall not eat of it, neither shall ye touch it, lest ye die.

The woman knew only what her husband, (Genesis 2:16, 17), had told her.

And the serpent said unto the woman, Ye shall not surely die: for God doth know that in the day ye eat thereof, then your eyes shall be opened, and ye shall be as Gods, knowing good and evil.

The serpent had witnessed God instruct Adam not to eat from the forbidden Tree, (Genesis 2:17), and knew that God wished to protect them from the knowledge of evil.

And when the woman saw that the tree was good for food, and that it was pleasant to the eyes, and a tree to be desired to make one wise, she took of the fruit thereof, and did eat, and gave also unto her husband with her; and he did eat.

The woman was mesmerized by the possibility of being equal to God.

And the eyes of them both were opened, and they knew that they were naked; and they sewed fig leaves together, and made themselves aprons.

The reality of what the man and woman had done struck them immediately.

And they heard the Voice of the LORD God walking in the garden in the cool of the day: and Adam and his wife hid themselves from the presence of the LORD God amongst the trees of the garden.

God's Voice, which was usually music to their ears, now filled them with guilt.

And the LORD God called unto Adam, and said unto him, Where art thou?

God was soothing their anxiety.

And he said, I heard Thy Voice in the garden, and I was afraid, because I was naked; and I hid myself.

Adam wanted God to fix the situation.

And He said, Who told thee that thou wast naked? Hast thou eaten of the tree, whereof I commanded thee that thou shouldest not eat?

God expressed His sadness over what He knew they had done.

And the man said, The woman whom Thou gavest to be with me, she gave me of the tree, and I did eat.

Adam couldn't bear the thought of making his Creator sad, and so shifted the blame onto Eve.

And the LORD God said unto the woman, What is this that thou hast done? And the woman said, The serpent beguiled me, and I did eat.

Eve, likewise, shifted the blame onto the serpent.

And the LORD God said unto the serpent, Because thou hast done this, thou art cursed above all cattle, and above every beast of the field; upon thy belly shalt thou go, and dust shalt thou eat all the days of thy life: and I will put enmity between thee and the woman, and between thy seed and her seed; it shall bruise thy head, and thou shalt bruise his heel.

God's displeasure with the serpent resulted in permanent negative repercussions for it, and culminated in His defeating Satan on the Cross of Calvary, (John 19:30).

Unto the woman He said, I will greatly multiply thy sorrow and thy conception; in sorrow thou shalt bring forth children; and thy desire shall be to thy husband, and he shall rule over thee. And unto Adam He said, Because thou hast hearkened

unto the voice of thy wife, and hast eaten of the tree, of which I commanded thee, saying, Thou shalt not eat of it: cursed is the ground for thy sake; in sorrow shalt thou eat of it all the days of thy life; thorns also and thistles shall it bring forth to thee; and thou shalt eat the herb of the field; in the sweat of thy face shalt thou eat bread, till thou return unto the ground; for out of it wast thou taken: for dust thou art, and unto dust shalt thou return.

The punishment God assigned to each party helped them fully understand the enormous gravity of what they had done. Their diet would now also include the plant life which was previously consumed only by animals, (Genesis 1:29, 30).

And Adam called his wife's name Eve; because she was the mother of all living.

Adam hoped in Eve's Seed, (Genesis 3:15).

Unto Adam also and to his wife did the LORD God make coats of skins, and clothed them.

God personally saw to it that Adam and Eve did not continue to feel shame.

And the LORD God said, Behold, the man is become as one of Us, to know good and evil: and now, lest he put forth his hand, and take also of the tree of life, and eat, and live for ever: therefore the LORD God sent him forth from the garden of Eden, to till the ground from whence he was taken. So He drove out the man; and He placed at the east of the garden of Eden Cherubims, and a flaming sword which turned every way, to keep the way of the tree of life.

God knew that allowing them to eat from the Tree of Life would cause them to live eternally in a state of perpetual sadness.

Chapter 4

And Adam knew Eve his wife; and she conceived, and bare Cain, and said, I have gotten a man from the LORD. And she again bare his brother Abel. And Abel was a keeper of sheep, but Cain was a tiller of the ground.

Adam and Eve's first two sons, Cain and Abel, developed opposing inclinations.

And in process of time it came to pass, that Cain brought of the fruit of the ground an offering unto the LORD.

Their first son, Cain was proud of what he had produced with his own hands.

And Abel, he also brought of the firstlings of his flock and of the fat thereof. And the LORD had respect unto Abel and to his offering: but unto Cain and to his offering He had not respect. And Cain was very wroth, and his countenance fell.

He did not understand why Abel's offering was accepted instead of his.

And the LORD said unto Cain, Why art thou wroth? And why is thy countenance fallen? If thou doest well, shalt thou not be accepted? And if thou doest not well, sin lieth at the door. And unto thee shall be his desire, and thou shalt rule over him.

God was trying to redirect him.

And Cain talked with Abel his brother: and it came to pass, when they were in the field, that Cain rose up against Abel his brother, and slew him.

He allowed his anger to take over, resulting in the loss of his only brother.

And the LORD said unto Cain, Where is Abel thy brother? And he said, I know not: am I my brother's keeper?

Cain refused to take responsibility for what he had done.

And He said, What hast thou done? The voice of thy brother's blood crieth unto Me from the ground.

God was filled with anguish.

And now art thou cursed from the earth, which hath opened her mouth to receive thy brother's blood from thy hand; when thou tillest the ground, it shall not henceforth yield unto thee her strength; a fugitive and a vagabond shalt thou be in the earth.

God could not allow the earth to continue to sustain this violent man.

And Cain said unto the LORD, My punishment is greater than I can bear. Behold, Thou hast driven me out this day from the face of the earth; and from Thy Face shall I be hid; and I shall be a fugitive and a vagabond in the earth; and it shall come to pass, that every one that findeth me shall slay me.

Cain did not want to accept his punishment.

And the LORD said unto him, Therefore whosoever slayeth Cain, vengeance shall be taken on him sevenfold. And the LORD set a mark upon Cain, lest any finding him should kill him.

God wanted to protect him.

And Cain went out from the presence of the LORD, and dwelt in the land of Nod, on the east of Eden. And Cain knew his wife; and she conceived, and bare Enoch: and he builded a city, and called the name of the city after the name of his son, Enoch. And unto Enoch was born Irad: and Irad begat Mehujael: and Mehujael begat Methusael: and Methusael begat Lamech. And Lamech took unto him two wives: the name of the one was Adah, and the name of the other Zillah. And Adah bare Jabal: he was the father of such as dwell in tents, and of such as have cattle. And his brother's name was Jubal: he was the father of all such as handle the harp and organ. And Zillah, she also bare Tubal-cain, an instructor of every artificer in brass and iron: and the sister of Tubal-cain was Naamah. And Lamech said unto his wives, Adah and Zillah, Hear my voice; ye wives of Lamech, hearken unto my speech: for I have slain a man to my wounding, and a young man to my hurt. If Cain shall be avenged sevenfold, truly Lamech seventy and sevenfold.

Cain started a line of humans that lived in sin, pleasure and violence.

And Adam knew his wife again; and she bare a son, and called his name Seth: For God, said she, hath appointed me another seed instead of Abel, whom Cain slew. And to Seth, to him also there was born a son; and he called his name Enos: then began men to call upon the Name of the LORD.

A godly line of humans began with Adam and Eve's third son.

Chapter 5

This is the book of the generations of Adam. In the day that God created man, in the likeness of God made He him; male and female created He them; and blessed them, and called their name Adam, in the day when they were created.

God originally called both the first man and the first woman "Adam", meaning "red" in Hebrew, after the clay from which Adam was formed.

And Adam lived an hundred and thirty years, and begat a son in his own likeness, after his image; and called his name Seth: and the days of Adam after he had begotten Seth were eight hundred years: and he begat sons and daughters: and all the days that Adam lived were nine hundred and thirty years: and he died. And Seth lived an hundred and five years, and begat Enos: and Seth lived after he begat Enos eight hundred and seven years, and begat sons and daughters: and all the days of Seth were nine hundred and twelve years: and he died. And Enos lived ninety years, and begat Cainan: and Enos lived after he begat Cainan eight hundred and fifteen years, and begat sons and daughters: and all the days of Enos were nine hundred and five years: and he died. And Cainan lived seventy years, and begat Mahalaleel: and Cainan lived after he begat Mahalaleel eight hundred and forty years, and begat sons and daughters: and all the days of Cainan were nine hundred and ten years: and he died. And Mahalaleel lived sixty and five years, and begat Jared: and Mahalaleel lived after he begat Jared eight hundred and thirty years, and begat sons and daughters: and all the days of Mahalaleel were eight hundred ninety and five years: and he died. And Jared

lived an hundred sixty and two years, and he begat Enoch: and Jared lived after he begat Enoch eight hundred years, and begat sons and daughters: and all the days of Jared were nine hundred sixty and two years: and he died. And Enoch lived sixty and five years, and begat Methuselah: and Enoch walked with God after he begat Methuselah three hundred years, and begat sons and daughters: and all the days of Enoch were three hundred sixty and five years: and Enoch walked with God: and he was not; for God took him. And Methuselah lived an hundred eighty and seven years, and begat Lamech: and Methuselah lived after he begat Lamech seven hundred eighty and two years, and begat sons and daughters: and all the days of Methuselah were nine hundred sixty and nine years: and he died. And Lamech lived an hundred eighty and two years, and begat a son: and he called his name Noah, saying, This same shall comfort us concerning our work and toil of our hands, because of the ground which the LORD hath cursed. And Lamech lived after he begat Noah five hundred ninety and five years, and begat sons and daughters: and all the days of Lamech were seven hundred seventy and seven years: and he died. And Noah was five hundred years old: and Noah begat Shem, Ham, and Japheth.

This godly line of humans would last until right after the Flood.

Chapter 6

And it came to pass, when men began to multiply on the face of the earth, and daughters were born unto them, that the sons of God saw the daughters of men that they were fair; and they took them wives of all which they chose.

These women were unable to choose whom they married.

And the LORD said, My Spirit shall not always strive with man, for that he also is flesh: yet his days shall be an hundred and twenty years.

God was growing weary of the wickedness and degeneration that was rampant on the earth before the Flood.

There were giants in the earth in those days; and also after that, when the sons of God came in unto the daughters of men, and they bare children to them, the same became mighty men which were of old, men of renown.

These giants' fathers were not humans, but were demons, (Job 1:6), who had strayed from God's purpose, and who will be punished at the end of time, (Jude 1:6).

And GOD saw that the wickedness of man was great in the earth, and that every imagination of the thoughts of his heart was only evil continually. And it repented the LORD that He had made man on the earth, and it grieved Him at His Heart.

God could not bear to look upon the condition of the earth any longer.

And the LORD said, I will destroy man whom I have created from the face of the earth; both man, and beast, and the creeping thing, and the fowls of the air; for it repenteth Me that I have made them.

God had no choice but to rid the earth of all life.

But Noah found grace in the Eyes of the LORD. These are the generations of Noah: Noah was a just man and perfect in his generations, and Noah walked with God. And Noah begat three sons, Shem, Ham, and Japheth.

Noah and his sons were the last of the godly line that started with Seth, (Genesis 5:3-32).

The earth also was corrupt before God, and the earth was filled with violence. And God looked upon the earth, and, behold, it was corrupt; for all flesh had corrupted his way upon the earth.

The condition of the earth was completely hopeless.

And God said unto Noah, The end of all flesh is come before Me; for the earth is filled with violence through them; and behold, I will destroy them with the earth.

God revealed His plan to Noah.

Make thee an ark of gopher wood; rooms shalt thou make in the ark, and shalt pitch it within and without with pitch. And this is the fashion which thou shalt make it of: the length of the ark shall be three hundred cubits, the breadth of it fifty cubits, and the height of it thirty cubits. A window shalt thou make to the ark, and in a cubit shalt thou finish it above; and the door of the ark shalt thou set in the side thereof; with lower, second, and third stories shalt thou make it.

The instructions were given to Noah in order to make the ark completely secure during the coming flood.

And, behold, I, even I, do bring a flood of waters upon the earth, to destroy all flesh, wherein is the breath of life, from under heaven; and every thing that is in the earth shall die.

God gave Noah foresight into the future, (Genesis 7:10, Genesis 7:21, 22).

But with thee will I establish My covenant; and thou shalt come into the ark, thou, and thy sons, and thy wife, and thy sons' wives with thee. And of every living thing of all flesh, two of every sort shalt thou bring into the ark, to keep them alive with thee; they shall be male and female. Of fowls after their kind, and of cattle after their kind, of every creeping thing of the earth after his kind, two of every sort shall come unto thee, to keep them alive. And take thou unto thee of all food that is eaten, and thou shalt gather it to thee; and it shall be for food for thee, and for them.

In this way, God would preserve life.

Thus did Noah; according to all that God commanded him, so did he.

Noah's faith would serve as an example to future generations, (Hebrews 11:7).

Chapter 7

And the LORD said unto Noah, Come thou and all thy house into the ark; for thee have I seen righteous before Me in this generation. Of every clean beast thou shalt take to thee by sevens, the male and his female: and of beasts that are not clean by two, the male and his female. Of fowls also of the air by sevens, the male and the female; to keep seed alive upon the face of all the earth. For yet seven days, and I will cause it to rain upon the earth forty days and forty nights; and every living substance that I have made will I destroy from off the face of the earth.

The time had come for Noah to save his life and the lives of all those who entered the ark with him.

And Noah did according unto all that the LORD commanded him. And Noah was six hundred years old when the flood of waters was upon the earth.

Noah's obedience resulted in the continuation of the human species.

And Noah went in, and his sons, and his wife, and his sons' wives with him, into the ark, because of the waters of the flood. Of clean beasts, and of beasts that are not clean, and of fowls, and of every thing that creepeth upon the earth, there went in two and two unto Noah into the ark, the male and the female, as God had commanded Noah. And it came to pass after seven days, that the waters of the flood were upon the earth.

The animals knew that God was going to destroy the earth.

In the six hundredth year of Noah's life, in the second month, the seventeenth day of the month, the same day were all the fountains of the great deep broken up, and the windows of heaven were opened. And the rain was upon the earth forty days and forty nights.

The Flood was cataclysmic, and lasted until nothing on the face of the earth survived.

In the selfsame day entered Noah, and Shem, and Ham, and Japheth, the sons of Noah, and Noah's wife, and the three wives of his sons with them, into the ark; they, and every beast after his kind, and all the cattle after their kind, and every creeping thing that creepeth upon the earth after his kind, and every fowl after his kind, every bird of every sort. And they went in unto Noah into the ark, two

and two of all flesh, wherein is the breath of life. And they that went in, went in male and female of all flesh, as God had commanded him: and the LORD shut him in.

Noah and everyone with him inside the ark were safe.

And the flood was forty days upon the earth; and the waters increased, and bare up the ark, and it was lift up above the earth. And the waters prevailed, and were increased greatly upon the earth; and the ark went upon the face of the waters.

God sent His cherubims to protect the ark.

And the waters prevailed exceedingly upon the earth; and all the high hills, that were under the whole heaven, were covered. Fifteen cubits upward did the waters prevail; and the mountains were covered. And all flesh died that moved upon the earth, both of fowl, and of cattle, and of beast, and of every creeping thing that creepeth upon the earth, and every man: all in whose nostrils was the breath of life, of all that was in the dry land, died. And every living substance was destroyed which was upon the face of the ground, both man, and cattle, and the creeping things, and the fowl of the heaven; and they were destroyed from the earth: and Noah only remained alive, and they that were with him in the ark. And the waters prevailed upon the earth an hundred and fifty days.

And so ended the Pre-Flood Era.

Chapter 8

And God remembered Noah, and every living thing, and all the cattle that was with him in the ark: and God made a wind to pass over the earth, and the waters assuaged; the fountains also of the deep and the windows of heaven were stopped, and the rain from heaven was restrained; and the waters returned from off the earth continually: and after the end of the hundred and fifty days the waters were abated.

God had compassion on these helpless passengers.

And the ark rested in the seventh month, on the seventeenth day of the month, upon the mountains of Ararat.

The ark had floated for five months.

And the waters decreased continually until the tenth month: in the tenth month, on the first day of the month, were the tops of the mountains seen. And it came to pass at the end of forty days, that Noah opened the window of the ark which he had made: and he sent forth a raven, which went forth to and fro, until the waters were dried up from off the earth. Also he sent forth a dove from him, to see if the waters were abated from off the face of the ground; but the dove found no rest for the sole of her foot, and she returned unto him into the ark, for the waters were on the face of the whole earth: then he put forth his hand, and took her, and pulled her in unto him into the ark. And he stayed yet other seven days; and again he sent forth the dove out of the ark; and the dove came in to him in the evening; and, lo, in her mouth was an olive leaf plucked off: so Noah knew that the waters were abated from off the earth. And he stayed yet other seven days; and sent forth the dove; which returned not again unto him any more. And it came to pass in the six hundredth and first year, in the first month, the first day of the month, the waters were dried up from off the earth: and Noah removed the covering of the ark, and looked, and, behold, the face of the ground was dry.

Noah waited over four more months inside the ark before he ventured to look outside.

And in the second month, on the seven and twentieth day of the month, was the earth dried.

The Flood lasted a year and ten days total.

And God spake unto Noah, saying, Go forth of the ark, thou, and thy wife, and thy sons, and thy sons' wives with thee. Bring forth with thee every living thing that is with thee, of all flesh, both of fowl, and of cattle, and of every creeping thing that creepeth upon the earth; that they may breed abundantly in the earth, and be fruitful, and multiply upon the earth. And Noah went forth, and his sons, and his wife, and his sons' wives with him: every beast, every creeping thing, and every fowl, and whatsoever creepeth upon the earth, after their kinds, went forth out of the ark.

So began the Post-Flood Era.

And Noah builded an altar unto the LORD; and took of every clean beast, and of every clean fowl, and offered burnt offerings on the altar.

Noah expressed his thankfulness to God for sparing his life.

And the LORD smelled a sweet savour; and the LORD said in His Heart, I will not again curse the ground any more for man's sake; for the imagination of man's

heart is evil from his youth; neither will I again smite any more every thing living, as I have done.

God's promise would last through eternity.

While the earth remaineth, seedtime and harvest, and cold and heat, and summer and winter, and day and night shall not cease.

The cycle of the seasons would remind us of His promise.

Chapter 9

And God blessed Noah and his sons, and said unto them, Be fruitful, and multiply, and replenish the earth.

God wanted human life to flourish.

And the fear of you and the dread of you shall be upon every beast of the earth, and upon every fowl of the air, upon all that moveth upon the earth, and upon all the fishes of the sea; into your hand are they delivered. Every moving thing that liveth shall be meat for you; even as the green herb have I given you all things. But flesh with the life thereof, which is the blood thereof, shall ye not eat. And surely your blood of your lives will I require; at the hand of every beast will I require it, and at the hand of man; at the hand of every man's brother will I require the life of man. Whoso sheddeth man's blood, by man shall his blood be shed: for in the image of God made He man. And you, be ye fruitful, and multiply; bring forth abundantly in the earth, and multiply therein.

God commanded us to respect all life, starting at conception.

And God spake unto Noah, and to his sons with him, saying, And I, behold, I establish My covenant with you, and with your seed after you; and with every living creature that is with you, of the fowl, of the cattle, and of every beast of the earth with you; from all that go out of the ark, to every beast of the earth. And I will establish My covenant with you; neither shall all flesh be cut off any more by the waters of a flood; neither shall there any more be a flood to destroy the earth. And God said, This is the token of the covenant which I make between Me and you and every living creature that is with you, for perpetual generations: I do set My bow in the cloud, and it shall be for a token of a covenant between Me and the earth. And it shall come to pass, when I bring a cloud over the earth, that the bow shall be seen in the cloud: and I will remember My covenant, which is between Me and you and every living creature of all flesh; and the waters shall no more become a flood to destroy all flesh. And the bow shall be in the cloud; and I will look upon it, that I may remember the everlasting covenant between God and every living creature of all flesh that is upon the earth. And God said unto Noah, This is the token of the covenant, which I have established between Me and all flesh that is upon the earth.

The rainbow is a symbol of God's mercy.

And the sons of Noah, that went forth of the ark, were Shem, and Ham, and Japheth: and Ham is the father of Canaan. These are the three sons of Noah: and of them was the whole earth overspread.

From Noah's three sons descended today's entire human race.

And Noah began to be an husbandman, and he planted a vineyard: and he drank of the wine, and was drunken; and he was uncovered within his tent.

Noah partook of the produce of the ground, which was no longer cursed, (Genesis 8:21, 22), and which produced abundantly.

And Ham, the father of Canaan, saw the nakedness of his father, and told his two brethren without.

Ham shamed his father.

And Shem and Japheth took a garment, and laid it upon both their shoulders, and went backward, and covered the nakedness of their father; and their faces were backward, and they saw not their father's nakedness.

Shem and Japheth's kindness toward their father brought his blessing upon them, (Genesis 9:26, 27).

And Noah awoke from his wine, and knew what his younger son had done unto him. And he said, Cursed be Canaan; a servant of servants shall he be unto his brethren. And he said, Blessed be the LORD God of Shem; and Canaan shall be his servant. God shall enlarge Japheth, and he shall dwell in the tents of Shem; and Canaan shall be his servant.

Noah's cursing of Ham's son, Canaan, resulted in the eventual subjugation of Canaan's descendants, the Canaanites, (Genesis 10:15-18), by the descendants of Abram, who was a descendant of Shem, (Genesis 11:10-26).

And Noah lived after the flood three hundred and fifty years. And all the days of Noah were nine hundred and fifty years: and he died.

Noah was the last to possess the uncommon longevity of life passed down through the godly line of humans starting from Adam, (Genesis 5:3-32).

Chapter 10

Now these are the generations of the sons of Noah, Shem, Ham, and Japheth: and unto them were sons born after the flood. The sons of Japheth; Gomer, and Magog, and Madai, and Javan, and Tubal, and Meshech, and Tiras. And the sons of Gomer; Ashkenaz, and Riphath, and Togarmah. And the sons of Javan; Elishah, and Tarshish, Kittim, and Dodanim. By these were the isles of the Gentiles divided in their lands; every one after his tongue, after their families, in their nations. And the sons of Ham; Cush, and Mizraim, and Phut, and Canaan. And the sons of Cush; Seba, and Havilah, and Sabtah, and Raamah, and Sabtecha: and the sons of Raamah; Sheba, and Dedan. And Cush begat Nimrod: he began to be a mighty one in the earth. He was a mighty hunter before the LORD: wherefore it is said, Even as Nimrod the mighty hunter before the LORD.

Nimrod, a descendant of Ham, was renown for his extraordinary hunting ability.

And the beginning of his kingdom was Babel, and Erech, and Accad, and Calneh, in the land of Shinar. Out of that land went forth Asshur, and builded Nineveh, and the city Rehoboth, and Calah, and Resen between Nineveh and Calah: the same is a great city. And Mizraim begat Ludim, and Anamim, and Lehabim, and Naphtuhim, and Pathrusim, and Casluhim, (out of whom came Philstim), and Caphtorim. And Canaan begat Sidon his firstborn, and Heth, and the Jebusite, and the Amorite, and the Girgasite, and the Hivite, and the Arkite, and the Sinite, and the Arvadite, and the Zemarite, and the

Hamathite: and afterward were the families of the Canaanites spread abroad. And the border of the Canaanites was from Sidon, as thou comest to Gerar, unto Gaza; as thou goest, unto Sodom, and Gomorrah, and Admah, and Zeboim, even unto Lasha. These are the sons of Ham, after their families, after their tongues, in their countries, and in their nations. Unto Shem also, the father of all the children of Eber, the brother of Japheth the elder, even to him were children born. The children of Shem; Elam, and Asshur, and Arphaxad, and Lud, and Aram. And the children of Aram; Uz, and Hul, and Gether, and Mash. And Arphaxad begat Salah; and Salah begat Eber. And unto Eber were born two sons: the name of one was Peleg; for in his days was the earth divided; and his brother's name was Joktan.

And Joktan begat Almodad, and Sheleph, and Hazarmaveth, and Jerah, and Hadoram, and Uzal, and Diklah, and Obal, and Abimael, and Sheba, and Ophir, and Havilah, and Jobab: all these were the sons of Joktan. And their dwelling was from Mesha, as thou goest unto Sephar a mount of the east. These are the sons of Shem, after their families, after their tongues, in their lands, after their nations. These are the families of the sons of Noah, after their generations, in their nations: and by these were the nations divided in the earth after the flood.

The rapid repopulation of the earth by Noah's three sons resulted in the vast diversity of languages, cultures and people we have today.

Chapter 11

And the whole earth was of one language, and of one speech. And it came to pass, as they journeyed from the east, that they found a plain in the land of Shinar;

and they dwelt there. And they said one to another, Go to, let us make brick, and burn them thoroughly. And they had brick for stone, and slime had they for mortar. And they said, Go to, let us build us a city and a tower, whose top may reach unto heaven; and let us make us a name, lest we be scattered abroad upon the face of the whole earth.

The first people after the Flood did not trust God's promise to never again destroy the earth by flood.

And the LORD came down to see the city and the tower, which the children of men builded. And the LORD said, Behold, the people is one, and they have all one language; and this they begin to do: and now nothing will be restrained from them, which they have imagined to do.

God knew they could achieve anything they wanted to and was concerned for their well-being as well as the well-being of the earth.

Go to, let Us go down, and there confound their language, that they may not understand one another's speech. So the LORD scattered them abroad from thence upon the face of all the earth: and they left off to build the city. Therefore is the name of it called Babel; because the LORD did there confound the language of all the earth: and from thence did the LORD scatter them abroad upon the face of all the earth.

God put an abrupt end to their project.

These are the generations of Shem: Shem was an hundred years old, and begat Arphaxad two years after the flood: and Shem lived after he begat Arphaxad five hundred years, and begat sons and daughters. And Arphaxad lived five and thirty years, and begat Salah: and Arphaxad lived after he begat Salah four hundred and three years, and begat sons and daughters. And Salah lived thirty years, and begat Eber: and Salah lived after he begat Eber four hundred and three years, and begat sons and daughters. And Eber lived four and thirty years, and begat Peleg: and Eber lived after he begat Peleg four hundred and thirty years, and begat sons and daughters. And Peleg lived thirty years, and begat Reu: and Peleg lived after he begat Reu two hundred and nine years, and begat sons and daughters. And Reu lived two and thirty years, and begat Serug: and Reu lived after he begat Serug two hundred and seven years, and begat sons and daughters. And Serug lived thirty years, and begat Nahor: and Serug lived after he begat Nahor two hundred years, and begat sons and daughters. And Nahor lived nine and twenty years, and begat Terah: and Nahor lived after he begat Terah an hundred and nineteen years, and begat sons and daughters. And Terah lived seventy years, and begat Abram, Nahor, and Haran. Now these are the generations of Terah: Terah begat Abram, Nahor, and Haran; and Haran begat Lot. And Haran died before his father Terah in the land of his nativity, in Ur of the Chaldees. And Abram and Nahor took them wives: the name of Abram's wife was Sarai; and the name of Nahor's wife, Milcah, the daughter of Haran, the father of Milcah, and the father of Iscah. But Sarai was barren; she had no child. And Terah took Abram his son, and Lot the son of Haran his son's son, and Sarai his daughter in law, his son Abram's wife; and they went forth with them from Ur of the Chaldees, to go into the land of Canaan; and they came unto Haran, and

dwelt there. And the days of Terah were two hundred and five years: and Terah died in Haran.

Human lifespan started gradually diminishing as people continued to live in the harsher Post-Flood Era conditions. Human fertility did as well.

Chapter 12

Now the LORD had said unto Abram, Get thee out of thy country, and from thy kindred, and from thy father's house, unto a land that I will show thee: and I will make of thee a great nation, and I will bless thee, and make thy name great; and thou shalt be a blessing: and I will bless them that bless thee, and curse him that curseth thee: and in thee shall all families of the earth be blessed.

God's promise to Abram would last for eternity.

So Abram departed, as the LORD had spoken unto him; and Lot went with him: and Abram was seventy and five years old when he departed out of Haran. And Abram took Sarai his wife, and Lot his brother's son, and all their substance that they had gathered, and the souls that they had gotten in Haran; and they went forth to go into the land of Canaan; and into the land of Canaan they came.

Thus began Abram's journey to the Promised Land.

And Abram passed through the land unto the place of Sichem, unto the plain of Moreh. And the Canaanite was then in the land. And the LORD appeared unto Abram, and said, Unto thy seed will I give this land: and there builded he an altar unto the LORD, who appeared unto him.

God's appearance gave Abram strength.

And he removed from thence unto a mountain on the east of Bethel, and pitched his tent, having Bethel on the west, and Hai on the east: and there he builded an altar unto the LORD, and called upon the Name of the LORD. And Abram journeyed, going on still toward the south.

Abram would need still more strength to continue his journey, and so he called on the God who would guide him through it.

And there was a famine in the land: and Abram went down into Egypt to sojourn there; for the famine was grievous in the land. And it came to pass, when he was come near to enter into Egypt, that he said unto Sarai his wife, Behold now, I know that thou art a fair woman to look upon: therefore it shall come to pass, when the Egyptians shall see thee, that they shall say, This is his wife: and they will kill me, but they will save thee alive. Say, I pray thee, thou art my sister: that it may be well with me for thy sake; and my soul shall live because of thee.

Abram wished to conceal Sarai's identity as his wife in order to preserve his own life.

And it came to pass, that, when Abram was come into Egypt, the Egyptians beheld the woman that she was very fair. The princes also of Pharaoh saw her, and commended her before Pharaoh: and the woman was taken into Pharaoh's house. And he entreated Abram well for her sake: and he had sheep, and oxen, and he asses, and menservants, and maidservants, and she asses, and camels.

Sarai's beauty won her fame and Abram favor with Pharaoh.

And the LORD plagued Pharaoh and his house with great plagues because of Sarai Abram's wife.

God supernaturally intervened on Abram's behalf.

And Pharaoh called Abram, and said, What is this that thou hast done unto me? Why didst thou not tell me that she was thy wife? Why saidst thou, She is my sister? So I might have taken her to me to wife: now therefore behold thy wife, take her, and go thy way. And Pharaoh commanded his men concerning him: and they sent him away, and his wife, and all that he had.

Pharaoh anxiously pushed away the cause his household's plagues.

Chapter 13

And Abram went up out of Egypt, he, and his wife, and all that he had, and Lot with him, into the south. And Abram was very rich in cattle, in silver, and in gold.

Abram's wealth was due in part to Pharaoh's urgency to get rid of him.

And he went on his journeys from the south even to Bethel, unto the place where his tent had been at the beginning, between Bethel and Hai; unto the place of the altar, which he had made there at the first: and there Abram called on the Name of the LORD.

Again Abram petitioned God for strength.

And Lot also, which went with Abram, had flocks, and herds, and tents. And the land was not able to bear them, that they might dwell together: for their

substance was great, so that they could not dwell together. And there was a strife between the herdmen of Abram's cattle and the herdmen of Lot's cattle: and the Canaanite and the Perizzite dwelled then in the land.

The strife between Abram's herdsmen and Lot's herdsmen would call unneeded attention from the inhabitants of the land.

And Abram said unto Lot, Let there be no strife, I pray thee, between me and thee, and between my herdmen and thy herdmen; for we be brethren. Is not the whole land before thee? Separate thyself, I pray thee, from me: if thou wilt take the left hand, then I will go to the right; or if thou depart to the right hand, then I will go to the left.

Abram loved Lot.

And Lot lifted up his eyes, and beheld all the plain of Jordan, that it was well watered every where, before the LORD destroyed Sodom and Gomorrah, even as the garden of the LORD, like the land of Egypt, as thou comest unto Zoar. Then Lot chose him all the plain of Jordan; and Lot journeyed east: and they separated themselves the one from the other.

The Jordan River Valley could be compared to the garden of Eden, (Genesis 2:8).

Abram dwelled in the land of Canaan, and Lot dwelled in the cities of the plain, and pitched his tent toward Sodom. But the men of Sodom were wicked and sinners before the LORD exceedingly.

Lot's choice to settle in Sodom would later cost him his wife, (Genesis 19:26).

And the LORD said unto Abram, after that Lot was separated from him, Lift up now thine eyes, and look from the place where thou art northward, and southward, and eastward, and westward: for all the land which thou seest, to thee will I give it, and to thy seed for ever. And I will make thy seed as the dust of the earth: so that if a man can number the dust of the earth, then shall thy seed also be numbered. Arise, walk through the land in the length of it and in the breadth of it; for I will give it unto thee. Then Abram removed his tent, and came and dwelt in the plain of Mamre, which is in Hebron, and built there an altar unto the LORD.

God's promises to him filled him with gratitude.

Chapter 14

And it came to pass in the days of Amraphel king of Shinar, Arioch king of Ellasar, Chedorlaomer king of Elam, and Tidal king of nations; that these made war with Bera king of Sodom, and with Birsha king of Gomorrah, Shinab king of Admah, and Shemeber king of Zeboiim, and the king of Bela, which is Zoar. All these were joined together in the vale of Siddim, which is the salt sea. Twelve years they served Chedorlaomer, and in the thirteenth year they rebelled. And in the fourteenth year came Chedorlaomer, and the kings that were with him, and smote the Rephaims in Ashteroth Karnaim, and the Zuzims in Ham, and the Emims in Shaveh Kiriathaim, and the Horites in their mount Seir, unto Elparan, which is by the wilderness. And they returned, and came to Enmishpat, which is Kadesh, and smote all the country of the Amalekites, and also the Amorites, that dwelt in Hazezontamar.

Chedorlaomer's campaign to re-conquer his territory devastated the people of the Jordan River Valley.

And there went out the king of Sodom, and the king of Gomorrah, and the king of Admah, and the king of Zeboiim, and the king of Bela (the same is Zoar) and they joined battle with them in the vale of Siddim; with Chedorlaomer the king of Elam, and with Tidal king of nations, and Amraphel king of Shinar, and Arioch king of Ellasar; four kings with five. And the vale of Siddim was full of slimepits; and the kings of Sodom and Gomorrah fled, and fell there; and they that remained fled to the mountain. And they took all the goods of Sodom and Gomorrah, and all their victuals, and went their way. And they took Lot, Abram's brother's son, who dwelt in Sodom, and his goods, and departed.

Their effort to defend themselves was futile.

And there came one that had escaped, and told Abram the Hebrew; for he dwelt in the plain of Mamre the Amorite, brother of Eshcol, and brother of Aner: and these were confederate with Abram. And when Abram heard that his brother was taken captive, he armed his trained servants, born in his own house, three hundred and eighteen, and pursued them unto Dan. And he divided himself against them, he and his servants, by night, and smote them, and pursued them unto Hobah, which is on the left hand of Damascus. And he brought back all the goods, and also brought again his brother Lot, and his goods, and the women also, and the people.

Abram displayed brilliant military tactics.

And the king of Sodom went out to meet him after his return from the slaughter of Chedorlaomer, and of the kings that were with him, at the valley of Shaveh, which is the king's dale. And Melchizedek king of Salem brought forth bread and wine: and he was the priest of the most high God. And he blessed him, and said, Blessed be Abram of the most high God, Possessor of Heaven and earth: and blessed be the most high God, which hath delivered thine enemies into thy hand. And he gave him tithes of all. And the king of Sodom said unto Abram, Give me the persons, and take the goods to thyself.

Unlike the king of Sodom, Melchizedek knew from Whom Abram received his strength.

And Abram said to the king of Sodom, I have lift up mine hand unto the LORD, the most high God, the Possessor of Heaven and earth, that I will not take from a thread even to a shoelatchet, and that I will not take any thing that is thine, lest thou shouldest say, I have made Abram rich: save only that which the young men have eaten, and the portion of the men which went with me, Aner, Eshcol, and Mamre; let them take their portion.

Abram knew as well.

Chapter 15

After these things the word of the LORD came unto Abram in a vision, saying, Fear not, Abram: I am thy Shield, and thy exceeding great reward.

God was reassuring him.

And Abram said, Lord GOD, what wilt Thou give me, seeing I go childless, and the steward of my house is this Eliezer of Damascus? And Abram said, Behold, to me Thou hast given no seed: and, lo, one born in my house is mine heir.

Abram still felt empty.

And, behold, the word of the LORD came unto him, saying, This shall not be thine heir; but he that shall come forth out of thine own bowels shall be thine heir. And He brought him forth abroad, and said, Look now toward heaven, and tell the stars, if thou be able to number them: and He said unto him, So shall thy seed be.

God made a promise that was as beautiful and enduring as the night sky.

And he believed in the LORD; and He counted it to him for righteousness.

Abram's faith was rewarded with the eventual birth of Isaac, (Genesis 21:3).

And He said unto him, I am the LORD that brought thee out of Ur of the Chaldees, to give thee this land to inherit it.

God reminded Abram of how He had led him so far.

And he said, Lord GOD, whereby shall I know that I shall inherit it?

Abram could not fathom how he and his descendants would inherit this vast land.

And He said unto him, Take Me an heifer of three years old, and a she goat of three years old, and a ram of three years old, and a turtledove, and a young pigeon. And he took unto him all these, and divided them in the midst, and laid each piece one against another: but the birds divided he not. And when the fowls came down upon the carcases, Abram drove them away.

God was using this ritual to show how impossible it is for Him to break His promise: if His promise could ever be broken, then God Himself would be divided in two like the animals Abram had sacrificed. His promise still stands today, and was proved to us on the Cross, where even in death, not one of His Bones was broken, (John 19:36).

And when the sun was going down, a deep sleep fell upon Abram; and, lo, an horror of great darkness fell upon him.

God was trying to reveal to Abram something of great gravity.

And He said unto Abram, Know of a surety that thy seed shall be a stranger in a land that is not theirs, and shall serve them; and they shall afflict them four hundred years; and also that nation, whom they shall serve, will I judge: and afterward shall they come out with great substance. And thou shalt go to thy fathers in peace; thou shalt be buried in a good old age. But in the fourth generation they shall come hither again: for the iniquity of the Amorites is not yet full.

God gave him foresight six hundred thirty-five years into the future, (Genesis 16:3, Genesis 16:16, Genesis 21:5, Genesis 25:26, Genesis 47:9, Exodus 12:40).

And it came to pass, that, when the sun went down, and it was dark, behold a smoking Furnace, and a burning Lamp that passed between those pieces.

The display of God's glory was meant to discourage any doubt that might have risen in Abram's heart.

In the same day the LORD made a covenant with Abram, saying, Unto thy seed have I given this land, from the river of Egypt unto the great river, the river

Euphrates: the Kenites, and the Kenizzites, and the Kadmonites, and the Hittites, and the Perizzites, and the Rephaims, and the Amorites, and the Canaanites, and the Girgashites, and the Jebusites.

The vision that God gave to Abram of his future home was glorious.

Chapter 16

Now Sarai Abram's wife bare him no children: and she had an handmaid, an Egyptian, whose name was Hagar. And Sarai said unto Abram, Behold now, the LORD hath restrained me from bearing: I pray thee, go in unto my maid; it may be that I may obtain children by her. And Abram hearkened to the voice of Sarai. And Sarai Abram's wife took Hagar her maid the Egyptian, after Abram had dwelt ten years in the land of Canaan, and gave her to her husband Abram to be his wife. And he went in unto Hagar, and she conceived: and when she saw that she had conceived, her mistress was despised in her eyes. And Sarai said unto Abram, My wrong be upon thee: I have given my maid into thy bosom; and when she saw that she had conceived, I was despised in her eyes: the LORD judge between me and thee.

Abram and Sarai's decision brought unbearable grief to their household.

But Abram said unto Sarai, Behold, thy maid is in thy hand; do to her as it pleaseth thee. And when Sarai dealt hardly with her, she fled from her face.

Abram did not possess the courage to reprimand Hagar, and so had Sarai carry her own will out when dealing with Hagar.

And the Angel of the LORD found her by a fountain of water in the wilderness, by the fountain in the way to Shur. And He said, Hagar, Sarai's maid, whence camest thou? And whither wilt thou go? And she said, I flee from the face of my mistress Sarai. And the Angel of the LORD said unto her, Return to thy mistress, and submit thyself under her hands.

God comforted Hagar and gave her courage to return and to face Sarai.

And the Angel of the LORD said unto her, I will multiply thy seed exceedingly, that it shall not be numbered for multitude. And the Angel of the LORD said unto her, Behold, thou art with child, and shalt bear a son, and shalt call his name Ishmael; because the LORD hath heard thy affliction. And he will be a wild man; his hand will be against every man, and every man's hand against him; and he shall dwell in the presence of all his brethren.

God made Hagar a promise that filled her with hope, then gave her foresight into the future, (Genesis 25:12-18).

And she called the Name of the LORD that spake unto her, Thou God Seest Me: for she said, Have I also here looked after Him that seeth me? Wherefore the well was called Beerlahai-roi; behold, it is between Kadesh and Bered.

Hagar responded by gratefully acknowledging God's watching over her, and commemorated the place of her encounter with Him.

And Hagar bare Abram a son: and Abram called his son's name, which Hagar bare, Ishmael.

Her obedience to God would be rewarded in the future, (Genesis 17:20).

And Abram was fourscore and six years old, when Hagar bare Ishmael to Abram.

And when Abram was ninety years old and nine, the LORD appeared to Abram, and said unto him, I am the Almighty God; walk before Me, and be thou perfect. And I will make My covenant between Me and thee, and will multiply thee exceedingly.

Neither the birth of Ishmael, nor the passage of thirteen years changed what God promised to do for Abram.

And Abram fell on his face:

Abram, now almost one hundred years old, could not comprehend how God's promises could be real.

and God talked with him, saying, As for Me, behold, My covenant is with thee, and thou shalt be a father of many nations. Neither shall thy name any more be called Abram, but thy name shall be Abraham; for a father of many nations have I made thee. And I will make thee exceeding fruitful, and I will make nations of thee, and kings shall come out of thee.

God was again giving Abram foresight into the future. He helped make it real for him by changing his name to Abraham, which, in Hebrew, means "Father of a Multitude". Abram was now Abraham, and would one day be the proud forefather of the King of Kings, (Matthew 1:1).

And I will establish My covenant between Me and thee and thy seed after thee in their generations for an everlasting covenant, to be a God unto thee, and to

thy seed after thee. And I will give unto thee, and to thy seed after thee, the land wherein thou art a stranger, all the land of Canaan, for an everlasting possession; and I will be their God.

God's promise to Abraham was meant to last for eternity.

And God said unto Abraham, Thou shalt keep My covenant therefore, thou, and thy seed after thee in their generations. This is My covenant, which ye shall keep, between Me and thee and thy seed after thee; every man child among thee shall be circumcised. And ye shall circumcise the flesh of your foreskin; and it shall be a token of the covenant betwixt Me and thee. And he that is eight days old shall be circumcised among thee, every man child in your generations, he that is born in the house, or bought with money of any stranger, which is not of thy seed. He that is born in thy house, and he that is bought with thy money, must needs be circumcised: and My covenant shall be in your flesh for an everlasting covenant. And the uncircumcised man child whose flesh of his foreskin is not circumcised, that soul shall be cut off from his people; he hath broken My covenant.

This ritual, which was to be carried out at infancy, would provide a physical trait that would set Abraham's descendants apart from the rest of the world for special use.

And God said unto Abraham, As for Sarai thy wife, thou shalt not call her name Sarai, but Sarah shall her name be. And I will bless her, and give thee a son also of her: yea, I will bless her, and she shall be a mother of nations; kings of people shall be of her.

God's promises were also to Sarai, the wife of Abraham's youth, who was now Sarah, which is Hebrew for "Princess".

Then Abraham fell upon his face, and laughed, and said in his heart, Shall a child be born unto him that is an hundred years old? And shall Sarah, that is ninety years old, bear?

Sarah no longer had the ability to bear children.

And Abraham said unto God, O that Ishmael might live before thee!

Abraham wanted God's promises to be carried out through his son Ishmael, who was now thirteen years old, (Genesis 17:1).

And God said, Sarah thy wife shall bear thee a son indeed; and thou shalt call his name Isaac: and I will establish My covenant with him for an everlasting covenant, and with his seed after him.

God convicted Abraham and told him again the news.

And as for Ishmael, I have heard thee: behold, I have blessed him, and will make him fruitful, and will multiply him exceedingly; twelve princes shall he beget, and I will make him a great nation.

God did not forget His promise to Hagar, (Genesis 16:10).

But My covenant will I establish with Isaac, which Sarah shall bear unto thee at this set time in the next year. And He left off talking with him, and God went up from Abraham.

God provided a set time for which Abraham could watch expectantly.

And Abraham took Ishmael his son, and all that were born in his house, and all that were bought with his money, every male among the men of Abraham's house; and circumcised the flesh of their foreskin in the selfsame day, as God had said unto him. And Abraham was ninety years old and nine, when he was circumcised in the flesh of his foreskin. And Ishmael his son was thirteen years old, when he was circumcised in the flesh of his foreskin. In the selfsame day was Abraham circumcised, and Ishmael his son. And all the men of his house, born in the house, and bought with money of the stranger, were circumcised with him.

Abraham's obedience to God was proof of his faith, (Hebrews 11:8-10).

Chapter 18

And the LORD appeared unto him in the plains of Mamre: and he sat in the tent door in the heat of the day; and he lift up his eyes and looked, and, lo, three Men stood by him: and when he saw Them, he ran to meet Them from the tent door, and bowed himself toward the ground, and said, My Lord, if now I have found favour in Thy sight, pass not away, I pray Thee, from Thy servant: let a little water, I pray Thee, be fetched, and wash Your Feet, and rest Yourselves under the tree: and I will fetch a morsel of bread, and comfort Ye Your Hearts; after that Ye shall pass on: for therefore are Ye come to Your servant. And They said, So do, as thou hast said.

Hospitality was a part of Abraham's character.

And Abraham hastened into the tent unto Sarah, and said, Make ready quickly three measures of fine meal, knead it, and make cakes upon the hearth. And Abraham ran unto the herd, and fetched a calf tender and good, and gave it unto a young man; and he hasted to dress it. And he took butter, and milk, and the calf which he had dressed, and set it before Them; and he stood by Them under the tree, and They did eat.

Abraham offered the most sustaining refection he could.

And They said unto him, Where is Sarah thy wife? And he said, Behold, in the tent. And He said, I will certainly return unto thee according to the time of life; and, lo, Sarah thy wife shall have a son. And Sarah heard it in the tent door, which was behind him.

God let Abraham and Sarah know the miracle that would happen within nine months' time.

Now Abraham and Sarah were old and well stricken in age; and it ceased to be with Sarah after the manner of women. Therefore Sarah laughed within herself, saying, After I am waxed old shall I have pleasure, my lord being old also?

Sarah simply could not believe this to be true.

And the LORD said unto Abraham, Wherefore did Sarah laugh, saying, Shall I of a surety bear a child, which am old? Is any thing too hard for the LORD? At the time appointed I will return unto thee, according to the time of life, and Sarah shall have a son.

God was strengthening Abraham and Sarah's faith.

Then Sarah denied, saying, I laughed not; for she was afraid. And He said, Nay; but thou didst laugh.

She didn't want to confess her unbelief.

And the Men rose up from thence, and looked toward Sodom: and Abraham went with Them to bring Them on the way. And the LORD said, Shall I hide from Abraham that thing which I do; seeing that Abraham shall surely become a great and mighty nation, and all the nations of the earth shall be blessed in him? For I know him, that he will command his children and his household after him, and they shall keep the way of the LORD, to do justice and judgment; that the LORD may bring upon Abraham that which He hath spoken of him.

God shared His plans with Abraham because He knew that Abraham would always do his best to uphold God's laws.

And the LORD said, Because the cry of Sodom and Gomorrah is great, and because their sin is very grievous; I will go down now, and see whether they have done altogether according to the cry of it, which is come unto Me; and if not, I will know.

God did not want to destroy these cities if He did not have to.

And the men turned their faces from thence, and went toward Sodom: but Abraham stood yet before the LORD.

Abraham knew Lot was in danger.

And Abraham drew near, and said, Wilt Thou also destroy the righteous with the wicked? Peradventure there be fifty righteous within the city: wilt Thou also

destroy and not spare the place for the fifty righteous that are therein? That be far from Thee to do after this manner, to slay the righteous with the wicked: and that the righteous should be as the wicked, that be far from Thee: shall not the Judge of all the earth do right?

Abraham was calling on God's mercy to save his nephew.

And the LORD said, If I find in Sodom fifty righteous within the city, then I will spare all the place for their sakes.

God pitied Abraham.

And Abraham answered and said, Behold now, I have taken upon me to speak unto the Lord, which am but dust and ashes: peradventure there shall lack five of the fifty righteous: wilt Thou destroy all the city for lack of five? And He said, If I find there forty and five, I will not destroy it. And he spake unto Him yet again, and said, Peradventure there shall be forty found there. And He said, I will not do it for forty's sake. And he said unto Him, Oh let not the Lord be angry, and I will speak: peradventure there shall thirty be found there. And He said, I will not do it if I find thirty there. And he said, Behold now, I have taken upon me to speak unto the Lord: peradventure there shall be twenty found there. And He said, I will not destroy it for twenty's sake. And he said, Oh let not the Lord be angry, and I will speak yet but this once: peradventure ten shall be found there. And He said, I will not destroy it for ten's sake. And the LORD went His way, as soon as He had left communing with Abraham: and Abraham returned unto his place.

Abraham knew there was no one in those cities whose righteousness would prevent the coming destruction.

Chapter 19

And there came two angels to Sodom at even; and Lot sat in the gate of Sodom: and Lot seeing them rose up to meet them; and he bowed himself with his face toward the ground; and he said, Behold now, my lords, turn in, I pray you, into your servant's house, and tarry all night, and wash your feet, and ye shall rise up early, and go on your ways. And they said, Nay; but we will abide in the street all night. And he pressed upon them greatly; and they turned in unto him, and entered into his house; and he made them a feast, and did bake unleavened bread, and they did eat.

Lot knew of the serious danger that existed in this city.

But before they lay down, the men of the city, even the men of Sodom, compassed the house round, both old and young, all the people from every quarter: and they called unto Lot, and said unto him, Where are the men which came in to thee this night? Bring them out unto us, that we may know them.

These men were overcome by lust.

And Lot went out at the door unto them, and shut the door after him, and said, I pray you, brethren, do not so wickedly. Behold now, I have two daughters which have not known man; let me, I pray you, bring them out unto you, and do ye to

them as is good in your eyes: only unto these men do nothing; for therefore came they under the shadow of my roof.

Lot was willing to protect his guests at any cost.

And they said, Stand back. And they said again, This one fellow came in to sojourn, and he will needs be a judge: now will we deal worse with thee, than with them. And they pressed sore upon the man, even Lot, and came near to break the door.

The men attempted to sodomize him.

But the men put forth their hand, and pulled Lot into the house to them, and shut to the door. And they smote the men that were at the door of the house with blindness, both small and great: so that they wearied themselves to find the door.

Lot's guests revealed their supernatural power.

And the men said unto Lot, Hast thou here any besides? Son in law, and thy sons, and thy daughters, and whatsoever thou hast in the city, bring them out of this place: for we will destroy this place, because the cry of them is waxen great before the Face of the LORD; and the LORD hath sent us to destroy it.

They then revealed their mission to him.

And Lot went out, and spake unto his sons in law, which married his daughters, and said, Up, get you out of this place; for the LORD will destroy this city. But he seemed as one that mocked unto his sons in law.

His sons-in-law had lost their beliefs in God.

And when the morning arose, then the angels hastened Lot, saying, Arise, take thy wife, and thy two daughters, which are here; lest thou be consumed in the iniquity of the city. And while he lingered, the men laid hold upon his hand, and upon the hand of his wife, and upon the hand of his two daughters; the LORD being merciful unto him: and they brought him forth, and set him without the city.

They were given until the last possible moment to leave the city.

And it came to pass, when they had brought them forth abroad, that He said, Escape for thy life; look not behind thee, neither stay thou in all the plain; escape to the mountain, lest thou be consumed.

The coming destructive force would leave almost the entire valley completely lifeless.

And Lot said unto Them, Oh not so, my Lord: behold now, Thy servant hath found grace in Thy sight, and Thou hast magnified Thy mercy, which Thou hast shewed unto me in saving my life; and I cannot escape to the mountain, lest some evil take me, and I die: behold now, this city is near to flee unto, and it is a little one: oh, let me escape thither, (is it not a little one?) and my soul shall live.

Lot could not imagine living outside of a city.

And He said unto him, See, I have accepted thee concerning this thing also, that I will not overthrow this city, for the which thou hast spoken. Haste thee, escape thither; for I cannot do any thing till thou be come thither. Therefore the name of the city was called Zoar.

God agreed not to destroy this small city.

The sun was risen upon the earth when Lot entered into Zoar. Then the LORD rained upon Sodom and upon Gomorrah brimstone and fire from the LORD out of heaven; and He overthrew those cities, and all the plain, and all the inhabitants of the cities, and that which grew upon the ground.

God completely destroyed everything and everyone.

But his wife looked back from behind him, and she became a pillar of salt.

So powerful was the nuclear blast that a single glance from Lot's wife instantly evaporated all the water in her body.

And Abraham gat up early in the morning to the place where he stood before the LORD: and he looked toward Sodom and Gomorrah, and toward all the land of the plain, and beheld, and, lo, the smoke of the country went up as the smoke of a furnace.

What Lot's uncle expected had come about.

And it came to pass, when God destroyed the cities of the plain, that God remembered Abraham, and sent Lot out of the midst of the overthrow, when He overthrew the cities in the which Lot dwelt.

God spared Lot for Abraham's sake.

And Lot went up out of Zoar, and dwelt in the mountain, and his two daughters with him; for he feared to dwell in Zoar: and he dwelt in a cave, he and his two daughters.

The same sinful practices in Zoar which were in Sodom and Gomorrah gave Lot reason to suspect its soon annihilation.

And the firstborn said unto the younger, Our father is old, and there is not a man in the earth to come in unto us after the manner of all the earth: come, let us make our father drink wine, and we will lie with him, that we may preserve seed of our father. And they made their father drink wine that night: and the firstborn went in, and lay with her father; and he perceived not when she lay down, nor when she arose. And it came to pass on the morrow, that the firstborn said unto the younger, Behold, I lay yesternight with my father: let us make him drink wine this night also; and go thou in, and lie with him, that we may preserve seed of our father. And they made their father drink wine that night also: and the younger arose, and lay with him; and he perceived not when she lay down, nor when she arose. Thus were both the daughters of Lot with child by their father. And the firstborn bare a son, and called his name Moab: the same is the father of the Moabites unto this day. And the younger, she also bare a son, and called his name Benammi: the same is the father of the children of Ammon unto this day.

Lot's daughters carried the sinful lifestyle of Sodom with them.

Chapter 20

And Abraham journeyed from thence toward the south country, and dwelled between Kadesh and Shur, and sojourned in Gerar. And Abraham said of Sarah his wife, She is my sister: and Abimelech king of Gerar sent, and took Sarah.

Sarah, who would soon give birth to Isaac, could have been defiled.

But God came to Abimelech in a dream by night, and said to him, Behold, thou art but a dead man, for the woman which thou hast taken; for she is a man's wife.

God intervened supernaturally once again on Abraham's behalf.

But Abimelech had not come near her: and he said, Lord, wilt Thou slay also a righteous nation? Said he not unto me, She is my sister? And she, even she herself said, He is my brother: in the integrity of my heart and innocency of my hands have I done this.

Abimelech was appealing to God's justice.

And God said unto him in a dream, Yea, I know that thou didst this in the integrity of thy heart; for I also withheld thee from sinning against Me: therefore suffered I thee not to touch her.

God acknowledged Abimelech's innocence.

Now therefore restore the man his wife; for he is a prophet, and he shall pray for thee, and thou shalt live: and if thou restore her not, know thou that thou shalt surely die, thou, and all that are thine.

Abraham's honor was valuable to God.

Therefore Abimelech rose early in the morning, and called all his servants, and told all these things in their ears: and the men were sore afraid.

They knew about the power of the God whom Abraham served.

Then Abimelech called Abraham, and said unto him, What hast thou done unto us? And what have I offended thee, that thou hast brought on me and on my kingdom a great sin? Thou hast done deeds unto me that ought not to be done.

Abimelech was a godly non-Canaanite king.

And Abimelech said unto Abraham, What sawest thou, that thou hast done this thing?

Abimelech knew Abraham was a godly man as well, and wanted to know the reasons behind his actions.

And Abraham said, Because I thought, surely the fear of God is not in this place; and they will slay me for my wife's sake. And yet indeed she is my sister; she is the daughter of my father, but not the daughter of my mother; and she became my wife.

Abraham told a half-truth in order to preserve his life.

And it came to pass, when God caused me to wander from my father's house, that I said unto her, This is thy kindness which thou shalt shew unto me; at every place whither we shall come, say of me, He is my brother.

The half-truth that Sarah was Abraham's sister was fabricated by Abraham at the very beginning of their journey to Canaan from Ur.

And Abimelech took sheep, and oxen, and menservants, and womenservants, and gave them unto Abraham, and restored him Sarah his wife. And Abimelech said, Behold, my land is before thee: dwell where it pleaseth thee.

Abimelech understood the position Abraham was in and showed him great kindness.

And unto Sarah he said, Behold, I have given thy brother a thousand pieces of silver: behold, he is to thee a covering of the eyes, unto all that are with thee, and with all other: thus she was reproved.

Abimelech admonished Sarah for having gone along with Abraham's deceitful plan.

So Abraham prayed unto God: and God healed Abimelech, and his wife, and his maidservants; and they bare children. For the LORD had fast closed up all the wombs of the house of Abimelech, because of Sarah Abraham's wife.

So serious was it for anyone to defile Abraham's wife, that it would have resulted in the discontinuation of their family line.

Chapter 21

And the LORD visited Sarah as He had said, and the LORD did unto Sarah as He had spoken. For Sarah conceived, and bare Abraham a son in his old age, at the set time of which God had spoken to him.

God's promise to Abraham and Sarah was fulfilled, (Genesis 17:19, 21).

And Abraham called the name of his son that was born unto him, whom Sarah bare to him, Isaac. And Abraham circumcised his son Isaac being eight days old, as God had commanded him. And Abraham was an hundred years old, when his son Isaac was born unto him.

Abraham continued to show faith through obedience to God.

And Sarah said, God hath made me to laugh, so that all that hear will laugh with me.

Their new son was a source of joy to Sarah.

And she said, Who would have said unto Abraham, that Sarah should have given children suck? For I have born him a son in his old age.

Sarah learned a valuable lesson about believing what God said, (Genesis 18:12).

And the child grew, and was weaned: and Abraham made a great feast the same day that Isaac was weaned.

Each stage in this special child's life was celebrated with joy.

And Sarah saw the son of Hagar the Egyptian, which she had born unto Abraham, mocking. Wherefore she said unto Abraham, Cast out this bondwoman and her son: for the son of this bondwoman shall not be heir with my son, even with Isaac. And the thing was very grievous in Abraham's sight because of his son.

Sarah and Abraham's decision, (Genesis 16:1-3), began again to bring grief to their house.

And God said unto Abraham, Let it not be grievous in thy sight because of the lad, and because of thy bondwoman; in all that Sarah hath said unto thee, hearken unto her voice; for in Isaac shall thy seed be called. And also of the son of the bondwoman will I make a nation, because he is thy seed.

God reminded Abraham of the promise He had made to Hagar, (Genesis 16:10).

And Abraham rose up early in the morning, and took bread, and a bottle of water, and gave it unto Hagar, putting it on her shoulder, and the child, and sent her away: and she departed, and wandered in the wilderness of Beersheba.

Abraham provided the best he could for his departing wife and son.

And the water was spent in the bottle, and she cast the child under one of the shrubs. And she went, and sat her down over against him a good way off, as it were a bowshot: for she said, Let me not see the death of the child. And she sat over against him, and lift up her voice, and wept.

Hagar had lost hope that Ishmael would continue to live.

And God heard the voice of the lad; and the Angel of God called to Hagar out of heaven, and said unto her, What aileth thee, Hagar? Fear not; for God hath heard the voice of the lad where he is.

God was still watching over Hagar and her son, (Genesis 16:13).

Arise, lift up the lad, and hold him in thine hand; for I will make him a great nation.

God reminded her as well of His promise to her, (Genesis 16:10).

And God opened her eyes, and she saw a well of water; and she went, and filled the bottle with water, and gave the lad drink. And God was with the lad; and he grew, and dwelt in the wilderness, and became an archer. And he dwelt in the wilderness of Paran: and his mother took him a wife out of the land of Egypt.

God provided for them and continued to do so throughout the child's life, all the way until adulthood, giving Hagar reassurance that what He said would come true, (Genesis 16:10-12).

And it came to pass at that time, that Abimelech and Phichol the chief captain of his host spake unto Abraham, saying, God is with thee in all that thou doest: now therefore swear unto me here by God that thou wilt not deal falsely with me, nor with my son, nor with my son's son: but according to the kindness that I have done unto thee, thou shalt do unto me, and to the land wherein thou hast sojourned.

Abimelech recognized God's presence with Abraham and all who were with Abraham, and sought to reap God's blessing through him.

And Abraham said, I will swear.

Abraham remembered the kindness that Abimelech had shown him, (Genesis 20:14, 15), and vowed to repay him.

And Abraham reproved Abimelech because of a well of water, which Abimelech's servants had violently taken away. And Abimelech said, I wot not who hath done this thing: neither didst thou tell me, neither yet heard I of it, but today.

Abimelech was completely unaware of the violent act, which was unlike something the generous king would have allowed to happen, that his servants had committed.

And Abraham took sheep and oxen, and gave them unto Abimelech; and both of them made a covenant.

Abraham and Abimelech were now confederate, in the same way Abraham had been confederate with Mamre the Amorite and his brothers during his stay in Hebron, (Genesis 14:13).

And Abraham set seven ewe lambs of the flock by themselves. And Abimelech said unto Abraham, What mean these seven ewe lambs which thou hast set by themselves? And he said, For these seven ewe lambs shalt thou take of my hand, that they may be a witness unto me, that I have digged this well. Wherefore he called that place Beersheba; because there they sware both of them. Thus they made a covenant at Beersheba: then Abimelech rose up, and Phichol the chief captain of his host, and they returned into the land of the Philistines.

Abraham wanted to compensate for any hard feelings Abimelech or his servants might have had toward him from their struggle over the well, (Genesis 21:25), and to part ways with Abimelech as peacefully as possible in order to avoid any future confrontations.

And Abraham planted a grove in Beersheba, and called there on the Name of the LORD, the everlasting God.

This well would serve as an important reminder of his and Abimelech's covenant, (Genesis 21:27), in case he ever needed to call on Abimelech to aid him militarily, and Abraham once again petitioned the God who had honored his requests in the past, (Genesis 12:8, Genesis 13:4), for the fortitude needed in this relationship between he and Abimelech.

And Abraham sojourned in the Philistines' land many days.

Abraham's relationship with the Philistines was a peaceful one, and he was content to stay in their land for a long period of time.

Chapter 22

And it came to pass after these things, that God did tempt Abraham, and said unto him, Abraham: and he said, Behold, here I am. And He said, Take now thy son, thine only son Isaac, whom thou lovest, and get thee into the land of Moriah; and offer him there for a burnt offering upon one of the mountains which I will tell thee of.

God wanted to see if Abraham loved Him with all of his heart.

And Abraham rose up early in the morning, and saddled his ass, and took two of his young men with him, and Isaac his son, and clave the wood for the burnt offering, and rose up, and went unto the place of which God had told him. Then on the third day Abraham lifted up his eyes, and saw the place afar off. And Abraham said unto his young men, Abide ye here with the ass; and I and the lad will go yonder and worship, and come again to you. And Abraham took the wood of the burnt offering, and laid it upon Isaac his son; and he took the fire in his hand, and a knife; and they went both of them together.

Deciding to obey God in this matter was the hardest thing Abraham had ever done.

And Isaac spake unto Abraham his father, and said, My father: and he said, Here am I, my son. And he said, Behold the fire and the wood: but where is the lamb

for a burnt offering? **And Abraham said, My son, God will provide Himself a lamb for a burnt offering: so they went both of them together.**

Abraham could not bear to tell Isaac what God had asked him to do.

And they came to the place which God had told him of; and Abraham built an altar there, and laid the wood in order, and bound Isaac his son, and laid him on the altar upon the wood.

Isaac, once aware of the awful task his father was assigned, also decided to trust in God.

And Abraham stretched forth his hand, and took the knife to slay his son. And the Angel of the LORD called unto him out of heaven, and said, Abraham, Abraham: and he said, Here am I. And He said, Lay not thine hand upon the lad, neither do thou any thing unto him: for now I know that thou fearest God, seeing thou hast not withheld thy son, thine only son from Me.

God stayed Abraham from harming Isaac, and revealed to them His true intentions.

And Abraham lifted up his eyes, and looked, and behold behind him a ram caught in a thicket by his horns: and Abraham went and took the ram, and offered him up for a burnt offering in the stead of his son.

God used this experience to teach Abraham what He intended to do for humanity. The substitute sacrifice He provided for Abraham symbolized what He would one day become on our behalf, (John 1:29).

And Abraham called the name of that place Jehovahjireh: as it is said to this day, In the mount of the LORD it shall be seen.

Abraham understood what God was trying to teach him, and named that mountain "Jehovahjireh", which means "God Will Provide", in order to commemorate Him providing Himself one day as a Sacrifice for our sins on Calvary.

And the Angel of the LORD called unto Abraham out of heaven the second time, and said, By Myself have I sworn, saith the LORD, for because thou hast done this thing, and hast not withheld thy son, thine only son: that in blessing I will bless thee, and in multiplying I will multiply thy seed as the stars of the heaven, and as the sand which is upon the sea shore; and thy seed shall possess the gate of his enemies; and in thy seed shall all the nations of the earth be blessed; because thou hast obeyed My Voice.

Abraham's decision to obey God ensured that it would be through his Descendant that God would ultimately triumph over evil in the Person of Jesus Christ, (Matthew 1:2-16).

So Abraham returned unto his young men, and they rose up and went together to Beersheba; and Abraham dwelt at Beersheba.

Abraham could live out the rest of his days in peace.

And it came to pass after these things, that it was told Abraham, saying, Behold, Milcah, she hath also born children unto thy brother Nahor; Huz his firstborn, and Buz his brother, and Kemuel the father of Aram, and Chesed, and Hazo, and Pildash, and Jidlaph, and Bethuel. And Bethuel begat Rebekah: these eight Milcah did bear to Nahor, Abraham's brother. And his concubine, whose name was Reumah, she bare also Tebah, and Gaham, and Thahash, and Maachah.

God had also caused the family of Abraham's one remaining brother, (Genesis 11:27, 28), to prosper.

Chapter 23

And Sarah was an hundred and seven and twenty years old: these were the years of the life of Sarah.

Sarah's miraculous giving of birth to Isaac when she was past the age of childbearing, (Genesis 18:11), symbolized the miraculous immaculate conception of Jesus Christ, (Luke1:34), and she was therefore commemorated in Scripture, being the only woman whose age was recorded upon her death.

And Sarah died in Kirjatharba; the same is Hebron in the land of Canaan: and Abraham came to mourn for Sarah, and to weep for her.

Abraham shared an incredible bond with his wife, Sarah, as they had together through the years witnessed firsthand God work miraculously in their lives time and time again, (Genesis 12:17, Genesis 18:14, Genesis 20:18, Genesis 21:2).

And Abraham stood up from before his dead, and spake unto the sons of Heth, saying, I am a stranger and a sojourner with you: give me a possession of a buryingplace with you, that I may bury my dead out of my sight.

Although Abraham had prospered enormously, (Genesis 12:16, Genesis 13:2, Genesis 13:6), since leaving his home in Ur of the Chaldees, he still did not own the land on which he lived, (Genesis 20:15, Genesis 21:34), and needed a place where he could bury his deceased wife, Sarah.

And the children of Heth answered Abraham, saying unto him, Hear us, my lord: thou art a mighty prince among us: in the choice of our sepulchers bury thy dead; none of us shall withhold from thee his sepulcher, but that thou mayest bury thy dead.

The sons of Heth knew, as Abimelech did, (Genesis 21:22), that God was with Abraham, and that by showing kindness to Abraham they would also be blessed, (Genesis 12:3).

And Abraham stood up, and bowed himself to the people of the land, even to the children of Heth.

Abraham was filled with gratitude.

And he communed with them, saying, If it be your mind that I should bury my dead out of my sight; hear me, and entreat for me to Ephron the son of Zohar, that he may give me the cave of Machpelah, which he hath, which is in the end of his field; for as much money as it is worth he shall give it me for a possession of a buryingplace amongst you.

Abraham did not want to take possession of the cave in which he wished to bury Sarah without having paid the full price it was worth.

And Ephron dwelt among the children of Heth: and Ephron the Hittite answered Abraham in the audience of the children of Heth, even of all that went in at the gate of his city, saying, Nay, my lord, hear me: the field give I thee, and the cave that is therein, I give it thee; in the presence of the sons of my people give I it thee: bury thy dead.

Ephron graciously offered to let Abraham have it for no cost whatsoever.

And Abraham bowed down himself before the people of the land.

Abraham was touched by the kindness these people were showing him.

And he spake unto Ephron in the audience of the people of the land, saying, But if thou wilt give it, I pray thee, hear me: I will give thee money for the field; take it of me, and I will bury my dead there.

Abraham wanted to secure in his permanent possession the cave in which he would bury Sarah.

And Ephron answered Abraham, saying unto him, My lord, hearken unto me: the land is worth four hundred shekels of silver; what is that betwixt me and thee? Bury therefore thy dead.

Ephron understood that the bond he shared with Abraham was worth more than the price of the sepulcher.

And Abraham hearkened unto Ephron; and Abraham weighed to Ephron the silver, which he had named in the audience of the sons of Heth, four hundred shekels of silver, current money with the merchant.

Ephron had unwittingly mentioned the cost of the land that Abraham wished to retain in order to dissuade Abraham from paying for it, and was now unable to prevent Abraham from measuring out the exact price he had just named in front of everyone.

And the field of Ephron, which was in Machpelah, which was before Mamre, the field, and the cave which was therein, and all the trees that were in the field, that were in all the borders round about, were made sure unto Abraham for a possession in the presence of the children of Heth, before all that went in at the

gate of his city. And after this, Abraham buried Sarah his wife in the cave of the field of Machpelah before Mamre: the same is Hebron in the land of Canaan. And the field, and the cave that is therein, were made sure unto Abraham for a possession of a buryingplace by the sons of Heth.

Abraham was able to retain the land in his belonging and could now bury Sarah, the wife of his youth.

Chapter 24

And Abraham was old, and well stricken in age: and the LORD had blessed Abraham in all things.

Abraham had led a long, full life.

And Abraham said unto his eldest servant of his house, that ruled over all that he had, Put, I pray thee, thy hand under my thigh: and I will make thee swear by the LORD, the God of heaven, and the God of the earth, that thou shalt not take a wife unto my son of the daughters of the Canaanites, among whom I dwell: but thou shalt go unto my country, and to my kindred, and take a wife unto my son Isaac.

Abraham had witnessed the lifestyle practiced in the Canaanite cities God had destroyed, (Genesis 19), and did not want his son, Isaac, to suffer the same fate his nephew, Lot, had suffered by choosing a Canaanite wife, (Genesis 19:26).

And the servant said unto him, Peradventure the woman will not be willing to follow me unto this land: must I needs bring thy son again unto the land from whence thou camest?

This dedicated servant truly loved Abraham and his family, and instead of having ever begrudged not being heir to Abraham's possessions, (Genesis 15:2, 3), he served Abraham faithfully, and was now willing to go to great lengths in order to find a wife for Isaac.

And Abraham said unto him, Beware thou that thou bring not my son thither again. The LORD God of heaven, which took me from my father's house, and from the land of my kindred, and which spake unto me, and that sware unto me, saying, Unto thy seed will I give this land; He shall send His Angel before thee, and thou shalt take a wife unto my son from thence.

Abraham had heard how his brother Nahor's family had prospered, (Genesis 22:20-24), and was confident that God, who had been with him every step throughout his journey from Ur, would select a wife for Isaac from that household.

And if the woman will not be willing to follow thee, then thou shalt be clear from this my oath: only bring not my son thither again.

Abraham didn't want his son Isaac to return and settle in Ur, and thus reject God's promise to give him and his descendants the land of Canaan, (Genesis 13:14-17, Genesis 15:18-21, Genesis 17:8).

And the servant put his hand under the thigh of Abraham his master, and sware to him concerning that matter.

This most trustworthy of servants would not rest until he had finished this final assignment by his master.

And the servant took ten camels of the camels of his master, and departed; for all the goods of his master were in his hand: and he arose, and went to Mesopotamia, unto the city of Nahor.

He intended to impress to the utmost whomever he would encounter on his quest for a wife for Isaac.

And he made his camels to kneel down without the city by a well of water at the time of the evening, even the time that women go out to draw water.

Anyone who saw this impressive caravan would have an idea of the affluence of his master, Abraham, to whom it belonged.

And he said, O LORD God of my master Abraham, I pray Thee, send me good speed this day, and shew kindness unto my master Abraham. Behold, I stand here by the well of water; and the daughters of the men of the city come out to draw water: and let it come to pass, that the damsel to whom I shall say, Let down thy pitcher, I pray thee, that I may drink; and she shall say, Drink, and I will give thy camels drink also: let the same be she that Thou hast appointed for Thy servant Isaac; and thereby shall I know that Thou hast shewed kindness unto my master.

The servant was not looking for a random act of kindness, but rather an attitude of service that would let him see the character of whomever he was observing.

And it came to pass, before he had done speaking, that, behold, Rebekah came out, who was born to Bethuel, son of Milcah, the wife of Nahor, Abraham's brother, with her pitcher upon her shoulder. And the damsel was very fair to look upon,

a virgin, neither had any man known her: and she went down to the well, and filled her pitcher, and came up. And the servant ran to meet her, and said, Let me, I pray thee, drink a little water of thy pitcher.

Rebekah was an unmarried grandniece of Abraham's, and the servant noticed the family resemblance immediately.

And she said, Drink, my lord: and she hasted, and let down her pitcher upon her hand, and gave him drink. And when she had done giving him drink, she said, I will draw water for thy camels also, until they have done drinking. And she hasted, and emptied her pitcher into the trough, and ran again unto the well to draw water, and drew for all his camels.

This hospitality evidently ran in the family, (Genesis 18:1-5).

And the man wondering at her held his peace, to wit whether the LORD had made his journey prosperous or not.

The servant was stunned by her beauty as well as by her kindness.

And it came to pass, as the camels had done drinking, that the man took a golden earring of half a shekel weight, and two bracelets for her hands of ten shekels weight of gold;

He revealed his true purport with this generous move.

and said, Whose daughter art thou? Tell me, I pray thee: is there room in thy father's house for us to lodge in?

The servant could hardly conceal his joy.

And she said unto him, I am the daughter of Bethuel the son of Milcah, which she bare unto Nahor. She said moreover unto him, We have both straw and provender enough, and room to lodge in. And the man bowed down his head, and worshipped the LORD.

Rebekah's heartwarming answer was enough to convince the servant his prayer, (Genesis 24:12-14), had acquired God's blessing.

And he said, Blessed be the LORD God of my master Abraham, who hath not left destitute my master of His mercy and His truth: I being in the way, the LORD led me to the house of my master's brethren.

He rejoiced, giving God the credit for his journey's success.

And the damsel ran, and told them of her mother's house these things.

Rebekah could hardly contain her joy.

And Rebekah had a brother, and his name was Laban: and Laban ran out unto the man, unto the well. And it came to pass, when he saw the earring and bracelets upon his sister's hands, and when he heard the words of Rebekah his sister, saying, Thus spake the man unto me; that he came unto the man; and, behold, he stood by the camels at the well.

Laban, who would later prove to be dishonest, (Genesis 31:41), was not interested in the good news told to him by Rebekah, but in Abraham's immense wealth, of which he caught his first glimpse on his sister's hands and in her nose.

And he said, Come in, thou blessed of the LORD; wherefore standest thou without? For I have prepared the house, and room for the camels.

Laban could scarcely believe the incredible riches on this caravan, (Genesis 24:10).

And the man came into the house: and he ungirded his camels, and gave straw and provender for the camels, and water to wash his feet, and the men's feet that were with him.

Laban also showed courteous hospitality.

And there was set meat before him to eat: but he said, I will not eat, until I have told mine errand. And he said, Speak on.

So excited was the servant that food did not interest him, despite having just made the long journey from his home.

And he said, I am Abraham's servant. And the LORD hath blessed my master greatly; and he is become great: and He hath given him flocks, and herds, and silver, and gold, and menservants, and maidservants, and camels, and asses. And Sarah my master's wife bare a son to my master when she was old: and unto him hath he given all that he hath. And my master made me swear, saying, Thou shalt not take a wife to my son of the daughters of the Canaanites, in whose land I dwell: but thou shalt go unto my father's house, and to my kindred, and take a wife unto my son. And I said unto my master, Peradventure the woman will not follow me. And he said unto me, The LORD, before Whom I walk, will send His Angel with thee, and prosper thy way; and thou shalt take a wife for my son of my kindred, and of my father's house: then shalt thou be clear from this my oath, when thou comest to my kindred; and if they give not thee one, thou shalt be clear from my oath. And I came this day unto the well, and said, O LORD God of

my master Abraham, if now Thou do prosper my way which I go: behold, I stand by the well of water; and it shall come to pass, that when the virgin cometh forth to draw water, and I say to her, Give me, I pray thee, a little water of thy pitcher to drink; and she say to me, Both drink thou, and I will also draw for thy camels: let the same be the woman whom the LORD hath appointed out for my master's son. And before I had done speaking in mine heart, behold, Rebekah came forth with her pitcher on her shoulder; and she went down unto the well, and drew water: and I said unto her, Let me drink, I pray thee. And she made haste, and let down her pitcher from her shoulder, and said, Drink, and I will give thy camels drink also: so I drank, and she made the camels drink also. And I asked her, and said, Whose daughter art thou? And she said, The daughter of Bethuel, Nahor's son, whom Milcah bare unto him: and I put the earring upon her face, and the bracelets upon her hands. And I bowed down my head, and worshipped the LORD, and blessed the LORD God of my master Abraham, which had led me in the right way to take my master's brother's daughter unto his son.

The servant relayed the entire story to Laban, continuing to give God the ultimate credit, (Genesis 24:27).

And now if ye will deal kindly and truly with my master, tell me: and if not, tell me; that I may turn to the right hand, or to the left.

The servant did not wish to pressure the family into allowing Rebekah to leave with him.

Then Laban and Bethuel answered and said, The thing proceedeth from the LORD: we cannot speak unto thee bad or good. Behold, Rebekah is before thee, take her, and go, and let her be thy master's son's wife, as the LORD hath spoken.

Rebekah's brother and father saw God's Hand in everything the servant had told them, and without hesitation agreed to let her leave with him.

And it came to pass, that, when Abraham's servant heard their words, he worshipped the LORD, bowing himself to the earth.

The servant was filled with gratitude.

And the servant brought forth jewels of silver, and jewels of gold, and raiment, and gave them to Rebekah: he gave also to her brother and to her mother precious things.

Rebekah was now heiress to Abraham's incredible wealth.

And they did eat and drink, he and the men that were with him, and tarried all night; and they rose up in the morning, and he said, Send me away unto my master.

The servant was eager to return to his master with the girl.

And her brother and her mother said, Let the damsel abide with us a few days, at the least ten; after that she shall go.

Rebekah's family realized how much they were going to miss her.

And he said unto them, Hinder me not, seeing the LORD hath prospered my way; send me away that I may go to my master.

The servant would have felt guilty had he delayed any longer.

And they said, We will call the damsel, and inquire at her mouth. And they called Rebekah, and said unto her, Wilt thou go with this man? And she said, I will go.

She understood this was her destiny.

And they sent away Rebekah their sister, and her nurse, and Abraham's servant, and his men. And they blessed Rebekah, and said unto her, Thou art our sister, be thou the mother of thousands of millions, and let thy seed possess the gate of those which hate them.

In uttering this prophetic blessing, Rebekah's family made sure to let Rebekah know that she and those who belonged to her would always have a home with them; a comforting fact that she would remember when seeking asylum for her son, Jacob, from his brother, Esau, (Genesis 27:43, 44).

And Rebekah arose, and her damsels, and they rode upon the camels, and followed the man: and the servant took Rebekah, and went his way.

Rebekah, now a princess, no longer had to concern herself with the care of the animals, (Genesis 24:19, 20), but now, along with her maids, rode them instead.

And Isaac came from the way of the well Lahairoi; for he dwelt in the south country. And Isaac went out to meditate in the field at the eventide: and he lifted up his eyes, and saw, and, behold, the camels were coming.

Isaac had been expecting the soon return of the servant with his bride-to-be.

And Rebekah lifted up her eyes, and when she saw Isaac, she lighted off the camel.

Rebekah knew this was the man whom she was to be with.

For she had said unto the servant, What man is this that walketh in the field to meet us? And the servant had said, It is my master: therefore she took a veil, and covered herself. And the servant told Isaac all things that he had done.

The servant had kept his oath to Abraham, (Genesis 24:9).

And Isaac brought her into his mother Sarah's tent, and took Rebekah, and she became his wife; and he loved her: and Isaac was comforted after his mother's death.

Rebekah was welcome in her new family.

Chapter 25

Then again Abraham took a wife, and her name was Keturah.

Abraham made sure to fill the empty place in his son's heart, (Genesis 24:67), that his deceased wife, Sarah, had left upon her death before he married his third wife.

And she bare him Zimran, and Jokshan, and Medan, and Midian, and Ishbak, and Shuah. And Jokshan begat Sheba, and Dedan. And the sons of Dedan were Asshurim, and Letushim, and Leummim. And the sons of Midian; Ephah, and Epher, and Hanoch, and Abida, and Eldaah. All these were the children of Keturah.

God continued to bless Abraham.

And Abraham gave all that he had unto Isaac. But unto the sons of the concubines, which Abraham had, Abraham gave gifts, and sent them away from Isaac his son, while he yet lived, eastward, unto the east country.

Abraham made sure to avoid any future squabbles over his wealth.

And these are the days of the years of Abraham's life which he lived, an hundred threescore and fifteen years.

Abraham had journeyed for one hundred years, (Genesis 12:4).

Then Abraham gave up the ghost, and died in a good old age, an old man, and full of years; and was gathered to his people.

Abraham rested.

And his sons Isaac and Ishmael buried him in the cave of Machpelah, in the field of Ephron the son of Zohar the Hittite, which is before Mamre; the field which Abraham purchased of the sons of Heth:

Ishmael put aside any resentment he might have had from not having received Abraham's wealth, (Genesis 25:5), and joined his brother in burying their father.

there was Abraham buried, and Sarah his wife.

Abraham was with the wife of his youth.

And it came to pass after the death of Abraham, that God blessed his son Isaac; and Isaac dwelt by the well Lahairoi. Now these are the generations of Ishmael, Abraham's son, whom Hagar the Egyptian, Sarah's handmaid, bare unto Abraham: and these are the names of the sons of Ishmael, by their names,

according to their generations: the firstborn of Ishmael, Nebajoth; and Kedar, and Adbeel, and Mibsam, and Mishma, and Dumah, and Massa, Hadar, and Tema, Jetur, Naphish, and Kedemah: these are the sons of Ishmael, and these are their names, by their towns, and by their castles; twelve princes according to their nations.

God remembered His promises to Abraham, (Genesis 17:19, 20).

And these are the years of the life of Ishmael, an hundred and thirty and seven years: and he gave up the ghost and died; and was gathered unto his people. And they dwelt from Havilah unto Shur, that is before Egypt, as thou goest toward Assyria: and he died in the presence of all his brethren.

God also remembered His promise to Hagar, (Genesis 16:10-12).

And these are the generations of Isaac, Abraham's son: Abraham begat Isaac: and Isaac was forty years old when he took Rebekah to wife, the daughter of Bethuel the Syrian of Padanaram, the sister to Laban the Syrian.

Thus ends the story of Abraham, the father of God's people, and so begins the story of Isaac.

And Isaac entreated the LORD for his wife, because she was barren: and the LORD was entreated of him, and Rebekah his wife conceived.

Rebekah remained barren for twenty years, (Genesis 25:20, Genesis 25:26).

And the children struggled together within her; and she said, If it be so, why am I thus? And she went to inquire of the LORD. And the LORD said unto her, Two nations are in thy womb, and two manner of people shall be separated from

thy bowels; and the one people shall be stronger than the other people; and the elder shall serve the younger.

God gave Rebekah foresight into the future, (Genesis 36:43, 2 Samuel 8:14).

And when her days to be delivered were fulfilled, behold, there were twins in her womb. And the first came out red, all over like an hairy garment; and they called his name Esau.

The thick hair that covered this child's skin would suit him well in the coming years as he grew to be a man of the field, (Genesis 25:27).

And after that came his brother out, and his hand took hold on Esau's heel; and his name was called Jacob: and Isaac was threescore years old when she bare them.

Upon observing this behavior from their second son, Isaac and Rebekah named him Jacob, which is the Hebrew word for "Supplanter", a name he would live up to, (Genesis 25:29-34, Genesis 27:18-29).

And the boys grew: and Esau was a cunning hunter, a man of the field; and Jacob was a plain man, dwelling in tents.

These brothers developed profoundly different personalities.

And Isaac loved Esau, because he did eat of his venison: but Rebekah loved Jacob.

Isaac's taste for venison would lead him to unintentionally give the birthright blessing to his youngest son, resulting in hatred in their family and the eventual sending away of the son whom Rebekah loved, (Genesis 27:41-Genesis 28:5).

And Jacob sod pottage: and Esau came from the field, and he was faint: and Esau said to Jacob, Feed me, I pray thee, with that same red pottage; for I am faint: therefore was his name called Edom.

Similar to "Adam", (Genesis 5:2), Edom literally means "Red" in Hebrew.

And Jacob said, Sell me this day thy birthright. And Esau said, Behold, I am at the point to die: and what profit shall this birthright do to me? And Jacob said, Swear to me this day; and he sware unto him: and he sold his birthright unto Jacob.

Jacob's mother had told him what had been told to her while he was yet in her womb, (Genesis 25:23); he now sought to bring it about by his own means.

Then Jacob gave Esau bread and pottage of lentils; and he did eat and drink, and rose up, and went his way: thus Esau despised his birthright.

This act of giving up his birthright for one simple meal characterized Esau as the undiscerning and impulsive person that he was, (Genesis 27:41).

Chapter 26

And there was a famine in the land, beside the first famine that was in the days of Abraham. And Isaac went unto Abimelech king of the Philistines unto Gerar.

Isaac sought help in this difficult time from the Philistine king who had made a covenant with his father, Abraham, (Genesis 21:27).

And the LORD appeared unto him, and said, Go not down into Egypt; dwell in the land which I shall tell thee of:

The time had not yet come for Abraham's seed to suffer in Egypt, (Exodus 12:40).

sojourn in this land, and I will be with thee, and will bless thee; for unto thee, and unto thy seed, I will give all these countries, and I will perform the oath which I sware unto Abraham thy father; and I will make thy seed to multiply as the stars of heaven, and will give unto thy seed all these countries; and in thy seed shall all the nations of the earth be blessed; because that Abraham obeyed My Voice, and kept My charge, My commandments, My statutes, and My laws.

God established the Abrahemic covenant with Isaac, just as He had promised, (Genesis 17:21).

And Isaac dwelt in Gerar: and the men of the place asked him of his wife; and he said, She is my sister: for he feared to say, She is my wife; Lest, said he, the men of the place should kill me for Rebekah; because she was fair to look upon.

Isaac made the same mistake his father had made on two occasions, (Genesis 12:11-13, Genesis 20:2).

And it came to pass, when he had been there a long time, that Abimelech king of the Philistines looked out at a window, and saw, and, behold, Isaac was sporting with Rebekah his wife. And Abimelech called Isaac, and said, Behold, of a surety she is thy wife: and how saidst thou, She is my sister? And Isaac said unto him, Because I said, Lest I die for her.

Isaac no longer could conceal his love for Rebekah, the wife God had predestined for him, (Genesis 24).

And Abimelech said, What is this thou hast done unto us? One of the people might lightly have lien with thy wife, and thou shouldest have brought guiltiness upon us.

Unlike what Abraham had thought, (Genesis 20:11), Abimelech was a godly king.

And Abimelech charged all his people, saying, He that toucheth this man or his wife shall surely be put to death.

Abimelech honored the covenant he had made with Abraham, (Genesis 21:27).

Then Isaac sowed in that land, and received in the same year an hundredfold: and the LORD blessed him. And the man waxed great, and went forward, and grew until he became very great: for he had possession of flocks, and possession of herds, and great store of servants: and the Philistines envied him. For all the wells which his father's servants had digged in the days of Abraham his father, the Philistines had stopped them, and filled them with earth.

Isaac started to see God's promises, (Genesis 26:3, 4), be fulfilled right before his very eyes.

And Abimelech said unto Isaac, Go from us; for thou art much mightier than we. And Isaac departed thence, and pitched his tent in the valley of Gerar, and dwelt there. And Isaac digged again the wells of the water, which they had digged in the days of Abraham his father; for the Philistines had stopped them after the death of Abraham:

He acted in accordance with Abimelech's wishes to him and to Abraham, (Genesis 21:23).

and he called their names after the names by which his father had called them.

And Isaac's servants digged in the valley, and found there a well of springing water. And the herdmen of Gerar did strive with Isaac's herdmen, saying, The water is ours: and he called the name of the well Esek; because they strove with him. And they digged another well, and strove for that also: and he called the name of it Sitnah. And he removed from thence, and digged another well; and for that they strove not: and he called the name of it Rehoboth; and he said, For now the LORD hath made room for us, and we shall be fruitful in the land.

Isaac held fast to God's promises to him, (Genesis 26:3, 4).

And he went up from thence to Beersheba. And the LORD appeared unto him the same night, and said, I am the God of Abraham thy father: fear not, for I am with thee, and will bless thee, and multiply thy seed for My servant Abraham's sake.

God continued to assure Isaac.

And he builded an altar there, and called upon the Name of the LORD, and pitched his tent there: and there Isaac's servants digged a well.

Isaac's act of digging a well in this location, despite his previous attempts being sabotaged multiple times, (Genesis 26:18-21), showed that he continued to believe what God said.

Then Abimelech went to him from Gerar, and Ahuzzath one of his friends, and Phichol the chief captain of his army. And Isaac said unto them, Wherefore come ye to me, seeing ye hate me, and have sent me away from you? And they said, We saw certainly that the LORD was with thee: and we said, Let there be now an oath betwixt us, even betwixt us and thee, and let us make a covenant with thee; that thou wilt do us no hurt, as we have not touched thee, and as we have done unto thee nothing but good, and have sent thee away in peace: thou art now the blessed of the LORD.

These men had begun to see, as they had with Abraham, (Genesis 21:22-27), the blessing of God on Isaac, and now sought to form a covenant with him, as they had done with his father.

And he made them a feast, and they did eat and drink. And they rose up betimes in the morning, and sware one to another: and Isaac sent them away, and they departed from him in peace.

Isaac's political adeptness allowed him to finally be at peace with his Philistine observers.

And it came to pass the same day, that Isaac's servants came, and told him concerning the well which they had digged, and said unto him, We have found water. And he called it Shebah: therefore the name of the city is Beersheba unto this day.

This was possibly the seventh well Isaac's servants had dug since their sojourn in this area, (Genesis 26:18-25), and Isaac named it a Hebrew word meaning "seventh".

And Esau was forty years old when he took to wife Judith the daughter of Beeri the Hittite, and Bashemath the daughter of Elon the Hittite: which were a grief of mind unto Isaac and to Rebekah.

Esau's choice to marry these heathen women brought much grief to Rebekah, (Genesis 27:46).

Chapter 27

And it came to pass, that when Isaac was old, and his eyes were dim, so that he could not see, he called Esau his eldest son, and said unto him, My son: and he said unto him, Behold, here am I. And he said, Behold now, I am old, I know not the day of my death: now therefore take, I pray thee, thy weapons, thy quiver and thy bow, and go out to the field, and take me some venison; and make me savoury meat, such as I love, and bring it to me, that I may eat; that my soul may bless thee before I die.

Isaac planned on bestowing the birthright blessing onto Esau, the son whom he loved, (Genesis 25:28).

And Rebekah heard when Isaac spake to Esau his son. And Esau went to the field to hunt for venison, and to bring it. And Rebekah spake unto Jacob her son, saying, Behold, I heard thy father speak unto Esau thy brother, saying, Bring me venison, and make me savoury meat, that I may eat, and bless thee before the LORD before my death. Now therefore, my son, obey my voice according to that which I command thee.

Rebekah knew this was her only chance to ensure the birthright was passed down to Jacob, the son whom she loved, (Genesis 25:28).

Go now to the flock, and fetch me from thence two good kids of the goats; and I will make them savoury meat for thy father, such as he loveth: and thou shalt bring it to thy father, that he may eat, and that he may bless thee before his death.

Rebekah had lived with Isaac since they were newlyweds, and knew how to satisfy his taste for savory meat.

And Jacob said to Rebekah his mother, Behold, Esau my brother is a hairy man, and I am a smooth man: my father peradventure will feel me, and I shall seem to him as a deceiver; and I shall bring a curse upon me, and not a blessing.

Jacob knew the danger that would come with attempting to acquire Esau's birthright blessing through deception, (Genesis 27:41).

And his mother said unto him, Upon me be thy curse, my son: only obey my voice, and go fetch me them.

Rebekah was willing to secure the birthright blessing for her younger son no matter what the cost.

And he went, and fetched, and brought them to his mother: and his mother made savoury meat, such as his father loved. And Rebekah took goodly raiment of her eldest son Esau, which were with her in the house, and put them upon Jacob her younger son: and she put the skins of the kids of the goats upon his hands, and upon the smooth of his neck: and she gave the savoury meat and the bread, which she had prepared, into the hand of her son Jacob.

Rebekah knew how to completely eradicate any chance of Isaac recognizing Jacob.

And he came unto his father, and said, My father: and he said, Here am I; who art thou, my son? And Jacob said unto his father, I am Esau thy firstborn; I have done according as thou badest me: arise, I pray thee, sit and eat of my venison, that thy soul may bless me. And Isaac said unto his son, How is it that thou hast found it so quickly, my son? And he said, Because the LORD thy God brought it to me. And Isaac said unto Jacob, Come near, I pray thee, that I may feel thee, my son, whether thou be my very son Esau or not.

Jacob's voice, (Genesis 27:22), caused Isaac to be wary.

And Jacob went near unto Isaac his father; and he felt him, and said, The voice is Jacob's voice, but the hands are the hands of Esau. And he discerned him not, because his hands were hairy, as his brother Esau's hands: so he blessed him.

Rebekah's plan worked.

And he said, Art thou my very son Esau? And he said, I am. And he said, Bring it near to me, and I will eat of my son's venison, that my soul may bless thee. And he brought it near to him, and he did eat: and he brought him wine, and he drank. And his father Isaac said unto him, Come near now, and kiss me, my son.

Isaac employed two more tests to make sure this was Esau.

And he came near, and kissed him: and he smelled the smell of his raiment, and blessed him, and said, See, the smell of my son is as the smell of a field which the LORD hath blessed:

The sense of smell, our most powerful sense for triggering memories, is what convinced Isaac to finally consent and to bless Jacob.

therefore God give thee of the dew of heaven, and the fatness of the earth, and plenty of corn and wine: let people serve thee, and nations bow down to thee: be lord over thy brethren, and let thy mother's sons bow down to thee: cursed be everyone that curseth thee, and blessed be he that blesseth thee.

Passed down in this blessing was the original covenant God had made with Abraham, (Genesis 12:3).

And it came to pass, as soon as Isaac had made an end of blessing Jacob, and Jacob was yet scarce gone out from the presence of Isaac his father, that Esau his brother came in from his hunting. And he also had made savoury meat, and brought it unto his father, and said unto his father, Let my father arise, and eat of his son's venison, that thy soul may bless me.

Esau was unaware of the crime committed against him by his own mother and brother.

And Isaac his father said unto him, Who art thou? And he said, I am thy son, thy firstborn Esau. And Isaac trembled very exceedingly, and said, Who? Where is he that hath taken venison, and brought it me, and I have eaten of all before thou camest, and have blessed him? Yea, and he shall be blessed.

Once having given the birthright blessing, Isaac could not take it back.

And when Esau heard the words of his father, he cried with a great and exceeding bitter cry, and said unto his father, Bless me, even me also, O my father.

Esau felt remorse over having been careless with his birthright, (Genesis 25:32-34).

And he said, Thy brother came with subtlety, and hath taken away thy blessing.

Isaac realized what he had just done.

And he said, Is not he rightly named Jacob? For he hath supplanted me these two times: he took away my birthright; and, behold, now he hath taken away my blessing. And he said, Hast thou not reserved a blessing for me?

Esau expected his father to recognize him as the rightful recipient of the birthright blessing.

And Isaac answered and said unto Esau, Behold, I have made him thy lord, and all his brethren have I given to him for servants; and with corn and wine have I sustained him: and what shall I do now unto thee, my son?

Isaac longed to help Esau.

And Esau said unto his father, Hast thou but one blessing, my father? Bless me, even me also, O my father. And Esau lifted up his voice, and wept.

Esau understood that it was too late.

And Isaac his father answered and said unto him, Behold, thy dwelling shall be the fatness of the earth, and of the dew of heaven from above; and by thy sword shalt thou live, and shalt serve thy brother; and it shall come to pass when thou shalt have the dominion, that thou shalt break his yoke from off thy neck.

Isaac couldn't bear to see the son whom he loved in a destitute state, and so gave him foresight into the future, (2 Kings 8:20-22).

And Esau hated Jacob because of the blessing wherewith his father blessed him: and Esau said in his heart, The days of mourning for my father are at hand; then will I slay my brother Jacob.

Esau reasoned that if Jacob were dead, he would not be able to receive the birthright blessing.

And these words of Esau her elder son were told to Rebekah: and she sent and called Jacob her younger son, and said unto him, Behold, thy brother Esau, as touching thee, doth comfort himself, purposing to kill thee. Now therefore, my son, obey my voice; and arise, flee thou to Laban my brother to Haran; and tarry with him a few days, until thy brother's fury turn away; until thy brother's anger turn away from thee, and he forget that which thou hast done to him: then I will send, and fetch thee from thence: why should I be deprived also of you both in one day?

Rebekah understood there was little time left for Jacob to save his own life.

And Rebekah said to Isaac, I am weary of my life because of the daughters of Heth: if Jacob take a wife of the daughters of Heth, such as these which are of the daughters of the land, what good shall my life do me?

And Isaac called Jacob, and blessed him, and charged him, and said unto him, Thou shalt not take a wife of the daughters of Canaan. Arise, go to Padanaram, to the house of Bethuel thy mother's father; and take thee a wife from thence of the daughters of Laban thy mother's brother.

Rebekah knew that not only would Jacob be safe with her brother, Laban, but that he would also be able to make a life there.

And God Almighty bless thee, and make thee fruitful, and multiply thee, that thou mayest be a multitude of people; and give thee the blessing of Abraham, to thee, and to thy seed with thee; that thou mayest inherit the land wherein thou art a stranger, which God gave unto Abraham. And Isaac sent away Jacob: and he went to Padanaram unto Laban, son of Bethuel the Syrian, the brother of Rebekah, Jacob's and Esau's mother.

Isaac knew that Jacob was leaving his house for good.

When Esau saw that Isaac had blessed Jacob, and sent him away to Padanaram, to take him a wife from thence; and that as he blessed him he gave him a charge, saying, Thou shalt not take a wife of the daughters of Canaan; and that Jacob obeyed his father and his mother, and was gone to Padanaram; and Esau seeing that the daughters of Canaan pleased not Isaac his father; then went Esau unto Ishmael, and took unto the wives which he had Mahalath the daughter of Ishmael Abraham's son, the sister of Nebajoth, to be his wife.

Esau was hoping that there was still a chance for him to receive the birthright blessing.

And Jacob went out from Beersheba, and went toward Haran. And he lighted upon a certain place, and tarried there all night, because the sun was set; and he took of the stones of that place, and put them for his pillows, and lay down in that place to sleep. And he dreamed, and behold a ladder set up on the earth, and the top of it reached to heaven: and behold the angels of God ascending and

descending on it. And, behold, the LORD stood above it, and said, I am the LORD God of Abraham thy father, and the God of Isaac: the land whereon thou liest, to thee will I give it, and to thy seed; and thy seed shall be as the dust of the earth, and thou shalt spread abroad to the west, and to the east, and to the north, and to the south: and in thee and in thy seed shall all the families of the earth be blessed. And, behold, I am with thee, and will keep thee in all places whither thou goest, and will bring thee again into this land; for I will not leave thee, until I have done that which I have spoken to thee of.

God sent Jacob a magnificent dream assuring him that he would be safe, and that He would keep the promises passed down to him through the birthright, (Genesis 12:2, 3, Genesis 13:14-17, Genesis 15:18, Genesis 17:6-8, Genesis 22:17, 18, Genesis 26:3-5, Genesis 27:28, 29).

And Jacob awaked out of his sleep, and he said, Surely the LORD is in this place; and I knew it not. And he was afraid, and said, How dreadful is this place! This is none other but the house of God, and this is the gate of Heaven.

Jacob realized that God was indeed with him, and this filled him with awe.

And Jacob rose up early in the morning, and took the stone that he had put for his pillows, and set it up for a pillar, and poured oil upon the top of it. And he called the name of that place Bethel: but the name of that city was called Luz at the first.

Jacob commemorated the place of this encounter with God by naming it "Bethel", meaning "house of God" in Hebrew.

And Jacob vowed a vow, saying, If God will be with me, and will keep me in this way that I go, and will give me bread to eat, and raiment to put on, so that I come again to my father's house in peace; then shall the LORD be my God: and this stone, which I have set for a pillar, shall be God's house: and of all that Thou shalt give me I will surely give the tenth unto Thee.

Jacob made a covenant with God, vowing to forever serve and obey Him.

Chapter 29

Then Jacob went on his journey, and came into the land of the people of the east. And he looked, and behold a well in the field, and, lo, there were three flocks of sheep lying by it; for out of that well they watered the flocks: and a great stone was upon the well's mouth. And thither were all the flocks gathered: and they rolled the stone from the well's mouth, and watered the sheep, and put the stone again upon the well's mouth in his place. And Jacob said unto them, My brethren, whence be ye? And they said, Of Haran are we. And he said unto them, Know ye Laban the son of Nahor? And they said, We know him.

Jacob recognized these men to be from Haran.

And he said unto them, Is he well? And they said, He is well: and behold, Rachel his daughter cometh with the sheep. And he said, Lo, it is yet high day, neither is it time that the cattle should be gathered together: water ye the sheep, and go and feed them.

Jacob wanted to immediately start working for his uncle, Laban.

And they said, We cannot, until all the flocks be gathered together, and till they roll the stone from the well's mouth; then we water the sheep. And while he yet spake with them, Rachel came with her father's sheep: for she kept them. And it came to pass, when Jacob saw Rachel the daughter of Laban his mother's brother, and the sheep of Laban his mother's brother, that Jacob went near, and rolled the stone from the well's mouth, and watered the flock of Laban his mother's brother. And Jacob kissed Rachel, and lifted up his voice, and wept.

Jacob was relieved over having found his family and a place where he could settle down and make a life.

And Jacob told Rachel that he was her father's brother, and that he was Rebekah's son: and she ran and told her father.

Rachel could hardly believe this was happening.

And it came to pass, when Laban heard the tidings of Jacob his sister's son, that he ran to meet him, and embraced him, and kissed him, and brought him to his house. And he told Laban all these things. And Laban said to him, Surely thou art my bone and my flesh. And he abode with him the space of a month.

Laban was pleased to finally meet his nephew.

And Laban said unto Jacob, Because thou art my brother, shouldest thou therefore serve me for nought? Tell me, what shall thy wages be?

Laban recognized how valuable a worker Jacob was, and wanted him to stay as long as possible.

And Laban had two daughters: the name of the elder was Leah, and the name of the younger was Rachel. Leah was tender eyed; but Rachel was beautiful and well favoured. And Jacob loved Rachel; and said, I will serve thee seven years for Rachel thy younger daughter.

Jacob had loved Rachel since he first saw her at the well, (Genesis 29:10).

And Laban said, It is better that I give her to thee, than that I should give her to another man: abide with me.

Laban knew that Jacob would be able to provide for his daughter.

And Jacob served seven years for Rachel; and they seemed unto him but a few days, for the love he had to her.

Jacob's time spent with Laban's family only caused his love for Rachel to grow.

And Jacob said unto Laban, Give me my wife, for my days are fulfilled, that I may go in unto her. And Laban gathered together all the men of the place, and made a feast. And it came to pass in the evening, that he took Leah his daughter, and brought her to him; and he went in unto her. And Laban gave unto his daughter Leah Zilpah his maid for an handmaid.

Laban's deception of Jacob let Jacob know he would have to be careful from now on when dealing with Laban, (Genesis 31:41).

And it came to pass, that in the morning, behold, it was Leah: and he said to Laban, What is this thou hast done unto me? Did not I serve with thee for Rachel? Wherefore then hast thou beguiled me?

Jacob was heartbroken over not having been with the woman he loved.

And Laban said, It must not be so done in our country, to give the younger before the firstborn. Fulfil her week, and we will give thee this also for the service which thou shalt serve with me yet seven other years.

Laban knew Jacob would do anything for Rachel, and used that to his advantage.

And Jacob did so, and fulfilled her week: and he gave him Rachel his daughter to wife also. And Laban gave to Rachel his daughter Bilhah his handmaid to be her maid.

Jacob was sad about being taken advantage of by his own uncle.

And he went in also unto Rachel, and he loved also Rachel more than Leah, and served with him yet seven other years.

Jacob's love for Rachel made the time working for Laban seem to diminish, (Genesis 29:20).

And when the LORD saw that Leah was hated, He opened her womb: but Rachel was barren. And Leah conceived, and bare a son, and she called his name Reuben: for she said, Surely the LORD hath looked upon my affliction; now therefore my husband will love me. And she conceived again, and bare a son; and said, Because the LORD hath heard that I was hated, He hath therefore given me this son also: and she called his name Simeon. And she conceived again, and bare a son; and said, Now this time will my husband be joined unto me, because I have born him three sons: therefore was his name called Levi. And she conceived again, and bare a son: and she said, Now will I praise the LORD: therefore she called his name Judah; and left bearing.

God felt compassion towards Leah for being unloved by her husband.

Chapter 30

And when Rachel saw that she bare Jacob no children, Rachel envied her sister; and said unto Jacob, Give me children, or else I die.

Rachel understood Jacob loved her, but was ashamed of not having any children.

And Jacob's anger was kindled against Rachel: and he said, Am I in God's stead, who hath withheld from thee the fruit of the womb?

Jacob confessed his powerlessness to give Rachel what she wanted.

And she said, Behold my maid Bilhah, go in unto her; and she shall bear upon my knees, that I may also have children by her. And she gave him Bilhah her handmaid to wife: and Jacob went in unto her. And Bilhah conceived, and bare Jacob a son. And Rachel said, God hath judged me, and hath also heard my voice, and hath given me a son: therefore called she his name Dan. And Bilhah Rachel's maid conceived again, and bare Jacob a second son. And Rachel said, With great wrestlings have I wrestled with my sister, and I have prevailed: and she called his name Naphtali.

Rachel started a struggle between her sister and her that would last until the birth of Joseph, (Genesis 30:22-24).

When Leah saw that she had left bearing, she took Zilpah her maid, and gave her Jacob to wife. And Zilpah Leah's maid bare Jacob a son. And Leah said, A troop cometh: and she called his name Gad. And Zilpah Leah's maid bare Jacob

a second son. And Leah said, Happy am I, for the daughters will call me blessed: and she called his name Asher.

Leah did not want to lose her place of importance to her sister, whom she knew Jacob already loved more, (Genesis 29:30).

And Reuben went in the days of wheat harvest, and found mandrakes in the field, and brought them unto his mother Leah. Then Rachel said to Leah, Give me, I pray thee, of thy son's mandrakes. And she said unto her, Is it a small matter that thou hast taken my husband? And wouldest thou take away my son's mandrakes also? And Rachel said, Therefore he shall lie with thee tonight for thy son's mandrakes. And Jacob came out of the field in the evening, and Leah went out to meet him, and said, Thou must come in unto me; for surely I have hired thee with my son's mandrakes. And he lay with her that night.

Like her father, (Genesis 29:26, 27), Leah was also able to shrewdly get what she wanted.

And God hearkened unto Leah, and she conceived, and bare Jacob the fifth son. And Leah said, God hath given me my hire, because I have given my maiden to my husband: and she called his name Issachar. And Leah conceived again, and bare Jacob the sixth son. And Leah said, God hath endued me with a good dowry; now will my husband dwell with me, because I have born him six sons: and she called his name Zebulun.

Leah was satisfied with how many children she now had.

And afterwards she bare a daughter, and called her name Dinah.

Growing up in this turbulent family, this daughter would one day witness the havoc caused by her two older brothers, Simeon and Levi, (Genesis 34:25).

And God remembered Rachel, and God hearkened to her, and opened her womb. And she conceived, and bare a son; and said, God hath taken away my reproach: And she called his name Joseph; and said, The LORD shall add to me another son.

God felt compassion towards Rachel for never having given birth.

And it came to pass, when Rachel had born Joseph, that Jacob said unto Laban, Send me away, that I may go unto mine own place, and to my country. Give me my wives and my children, for whom I have served thee, and let me go: for thou knowest my service which I have done thee.

Jacob's time, (Genesis 29:27), that he had agreed to serve Laban was finished, and he was ready to return home.

And Laban said unto him, I pray thee, if I have found favour in thine eyes, tarry: for I have learned by experience that the LORD hath blessed me for thy sake. And he said, Appoint me thy wages, and I will give it.

Laban did not want to lose this valuable worker.

And he said unto him, Thou knowest how I have served thee, and how thy cattle was with me. For it was little which thou hadst before I came, and it is now increased unto a multitude; and the LORD hath blessed thee since my coming: and now when shall I provide for mine own house also?

Jacob was not interested in continuing to serve his deceptive uncle any longer than he had to.

And he said, What shall I give thee? And Jacob said, Thou shalt not give me any thing: if thou wilt do this thing for me, I will again feed and keep thy flock: I will pass through all thy flock today, removing from thence all the speckled and spotted cattle, and all the brown cattle among the sheep, and the spotted and speckled among the goats: and of such shall be my hire. So shall my righteousness answer for me in time to come, when it shall come for my hire before thy face: every one that is not speckled and spotted among the goats, and brown among the sheep, that shall be counted stolen with me.

Jacob remembered being deceived by Laban, (Genesis 29:19-27), and did not trust him to give him agreed upon wages, and so proposed his own method of payment.

And Laban said, Behold, I would it might be according to thy word.

Laban assumed Jacob's plan would benefit solely himself.

And he removed that day the he goats that were ringstraked and spotted, and all the she goats that were speckled and spotted, and every one that had some white in it, and all the brown among the sheep, and gave them into the hand of his sons. And he set three days' journey betwixt himself and Jacob: and Jacob fed the rest of Laban's flocks.

Laban sought to benefit as much as possible from this talented worker by having him tend only his flocks, leaving Jacob's new flocks under the tending of his own sons.

And Jacob took him rods of green poplar, and of the hazel and chestnut tree; and pilled white strakes in them, and made the white appear which was in the rods. And he set the rods which he had pilled before the flocks in the gutters in the watering troughs when the flocks came to drink, that they should conceive when they came to drink. And the flocks conceived before the rods, and brought forth cattle ringstraked, speckled, and spotted.

During Jacob's time working for Laban, he had learned how to manipulate the genetics of animals.

And Jacob did separate the lambs, and set the faces of the flocks toward the ringstraked, and all the brown in the flock of Laban; and he put his own flocks by themselves, and put them not unto Laban's cattle. And it came to pass, whensoever the stronger cattle did conceive, that Jacob laid the rods before the eyes of the cattle in the gutters, that they might conceive among the rods. But when the cattle were feeble, he put them not in: so the feebler were Laban's, and the stronger Jacob's. And the man increased exceedingly, and had much cattle, and maidservants, and menservants, and camels, and asses.

Jacob used this knowledge to his benefit.

Chapter 31

And he heard the words of Laban's sons, saying, Jacob hath taken away all that was our father's; and of that which was our father's hath he gotten all this glory. And Jacob beheld the countenance of Laban, and, behold, it was not toward him as before.

Laban and his sons realized Jacob had gotten the best of them, and resented him for it.

And the LORD said unto Jacob, Return unto the land of thy fathers, and to thy kindred; and I will be with thee.

God knew it was time for Jacob to return home.

And Jacob sent and called Rachel and Leah to the field unto his flock, and said unto them, I see your father's countenance, that it is not toward me as before; but the God of my father hath been with me. And ye know that with all my power I have served your father. And your father hath deceived me, and changed my wages ten times; but God suffered him not to hurt me. If he said thus, The speckled shall be thy wages; then all the cattle bare speckled: and if he said thus, The ringstraked shall be thy hire; then bare all the cattle ringstraked. Thus God hath taken away the cattle of your father, and given them to me.

Jacob explained to his wives that he believed he was justified in playing the trick on Laban.

And it came to pass at the time that the cattle conceived, that I lifted up mine eyes, and saw in a dream, and, behold, the rams which leaped upon the cattle were ringstraked, speckled, and grisled. And the Angel of God spake unto me in a dream, saying, Jacob: and I said, Here am I. And He said, Lift up now thine eyes, and see, all the rams which leap upon the cattle are ringstraked, speckled, and grisled: for I have seen all that Laban doeth unto thee. I am the God of Bethel, where thou anointedst the pillar, and where thou vowedst a vow unto Me: now arise, get thee out from this land, and return unto the land of thy kindred.

He continued to explain to them that God was behind everything he was doing.

And Rachel and Leah answered and said unto him, Is there yet any portion or inheritance for us in our father's house? Are we not counted of him strangers? For he hath sold us, and hath quite devoured also our money. For all the riches which God hath taken from our father, that is ours, and our children's: now then, whatsoever God hath said unto thee, do.

Laban's daughters acknowledged the abuse with which Laban had treated Jacob and themselves, and gave Jacob their support.

Then Jacob rose up, and set his sons and his wives upon camels; and he carried away all his cattle, and all his goods which he had gotten, the cattle of his getting, which he had gotten in Padanaram, for to go to Isaac his father in the land of Canaan. And Laban went to shear his sheep:

Jacob waited until Laban had left to shear his sheep to escape.

and Rachel had stolen the images that were her father's.

Rachel was unsatisfied with the amount of disrespect shown to her father by leaving without telling him, and sought to further spite him by stealing his gods. She also believed they would need their help in their flight from her father.

And Jacob stole away unawares to Laban the Syrian, in that he told him not that he fled. So he fled with all that he had; and he rose up, and passed over the river, and set his face toward the mount Gilead. And it was told Laban on the third day that Jacob was fled.

In removing himself three days' journey from Jacob, (Genesis 30:36), Laban had allowed Jacob a window of time in which to escape.

And he took his brethren with him, and pursued after him seven days' journey; and they overtook him in the mount Gilead.

Although he knew he deserved it, Laban did not want to lose his two daughters and his grandchildren.

And God came to Laban the Syrian in a dream by night, and said unto him, Take heed that thou speak not to Jacob either good or bad.

God intervened supernaturally on Jacob's behalf.

Then Laban overtook Jacob. Now Jacob had pitched his tent in the mount: and Laban with his brethren pitched in the mount of Gilead. And Laban said to Jacob, What hast thou done, that thou hast stolen away unawares to me, and carried away my daughters, as captives taken with the sword? Wherefore didst thou flee away secretly, and steal away from me; and didst not tell me, that I might have sent thee away with mirth, and with songs, with tabret, and with harp? And hast not suffered me to kiss my sons and my daughters? Thou hast now done foolishly in so doing.

Laban remembered his dream from the night before, and was sure not to reveal his true feelings to Jacob.

It is in the power of my hand to do you hurt: but the God of your father spake unto me yesternight, saying, Take thou heed that thou speak not to Jacob either good or bad. And now, though thou wouldest needs be gone, because thou sore longedst after thy father's house, yet wherefore hast thou stolen my gods?

Laban was only honest in two respects: the dream he had had the night before and his missing gods.

And Jacob answered and said to Laban, Because I was afraid: for I said, Peradventure thou wouldest take by force thy daughters from me.

Jacob confessed his distrust of Laban.

With whomsoever thou findest thy gods, let him not live: before our brethren discern thou what is thine with me, and take it to thee. For Jacob knew not that Rachel had stolen them.

Jacob was confident in his own integrity and the integrity of those with him.

And Laban went into Jacob's tent, and into Leah's tent, and into the two maidservants' tents; but he found them not. Then went he out of Leah's tent, and entered into Rachel's tent.

It was Jacob's practice to put Rachel in the most protected place, (Genesis 33:2), and her tent was the last Laban searched.

Now Rachel had taken the images, and put them in the camel's furniture, and sat upon them. And Laban searched all the tent, but found them not.

Rachel risked losing her life if she was found with the stolen gods.

And she said to her father, Let it not displease my lord that I cannot rise up before thee; for the custom of women is upon me. And he searched, but found not the images.

Rachel needed to provide a reason for not showing the customary respect of standing to greet one's father.

And Jacob was wroth, and chode with Laban: and Jacob answered and said to Laban, What is my trespass? What is my sin, that thou hast so hotly pursued after me? Whereas thou hast searched all my stuff, what hast thou found of all thy household stuff? Set it here before my brethren and thy brethren, that they may judge betwixt us both.

Jacob began to vent his frustration with Laban in front of his own family.

This twenty years have I been with thee; thy ewes and thy she goats have not cast their young, and the rams of thy flock have I not eaten. That which was torn of beasts I brought not unto thee; I bare the loss of it; of my hand didst thou require it, whether stolen by day, or stolen by night. Thus I was; in the day the drought consumed me, and the frost by night; and my sleep departed from mine eyes. Thus have I been twenty years in thy house; I served thee fourteen years for thy two daughters, and six years for thy cattle: and thou hast changed my wages ten times. Except the God of my father, the God of Abraham, and the Fear of Isaac, had been with me, surely thou hadst sent me away now empty. God hath seen mine affliction and the labour of my hands, and rebuked thee yesternight.

Jacob truthfully recounted everything that had happened between them, including God's intervention, (Genesis 31:24).

And Laban answered and said unto Jacob, These daughters are my daughters, and these children are my children, and these cattle are my cattle, and all that

thou seest is mine: and what can I do this day unto these my daughters, or unto their children which they have born? Now therefore come thou, let us make a covenant, I and thou; and let it be for a witness between me and thee.

Laban realized that he had been wrong for how he had treated his son-in-law.

And Jacob took a stone, and set it up for a pillar. And Jacob said unto his brethren, Gather stones; and they took stones, and made an heap: and they did eat there upon the heap.

Jacob memorialized the place of their covenant, and moreover shared a meal with Laban, which symbolized mutual peace, (Exodus 24:10, 11).

And Laban called it Jegarsahadutha: but Jacob called it Galeed. And Laban said, This heap is a witness between me and thee this day. Therefore was the name of it called Galeed;

Both Laban and Jacob named the place "Heap of witness", using their own languages.

and Mizpah; for he said, The LORD watch between me and thee, when we are absent one from another.

Laban wanted God to keep an Eye on them, and so named it "Watch tower".

If thou shalt afflict my daughters, or if thou shalt take other wives beside my daughters, no man is with us; see, God is witness betwixt me and thee.

Laban was concerned for his two daughters, whom he knew he would not see again.

And Laban said to Jacob, Behold this heap, and behold this pillar, which I have cast betwixt me and thee; this heap be witness, and this pillar be witness, that I

will not pass over this heap to thee, and that thou shalt not pass over this heap and this pillar unto me, for harm. The God of Abraham, and the God of Nahor, the God of their father, judge betwixt us.

Laban knew Jacob would grow to be a powerful nation, (Genesis 27:28, 29), and wanted to make sure there would be no conflict between them in the future.

And Jacob sware by the Fear of his father Isaac. Then Jacob offered sacrifice upon the mount, and called his brethren to eat bread: and they did eat bread, and tarried all night in the mount.

Jacob ratified the peace agreement.

And early in the morning Laban rose up, and kissed his sons and his daughters, and blessed them: and Laban departed, and returned unto his place.

Jacob's ordeal with Laban was over.

Chapter 32

And Jacob went on his way, and the angels of God met him. And when Jacob saw them, he said, This is God's host: and he called the name of that place Mahanaim.

Upon seeing the angels, Jacob understood his company was not traveling alone, and so named the place where he saw the angels Mahanaim, which means "Two camps" in Hebrew.

And Jacob sent messengers before him to Esau his brother unto the land of Seir, the country of Edom. And he commanded them, saying, Thus shall ye speak unto

my lord Esau; Thy servant Jacob saith thus, I have sojourned with Laban, and stayed there until now: and I have oxen, and asses, flocks, and menservants, and womenservants: and I have sent to tell my lord, that I may find grace in thy sight.

Jacob didn't know if his brother's anger had subsided, (Genesis 27:41), and was submissive in his approach in order to appease any anger he might still have been holding on to.

And the messengers returned to Jacob, saying, We came to thy brother Esau, and also he cometh to meet thee, and four hundred men with him.

Twenty years had passed, (Genesis 31:41), since Esau had last seen his twin.

Then Jacob was greatly afraid and distressed: and he divided the people that was with him, and the flocks, and herds, and the camels, into two bands; and said, If Esau come to the one company, and smite it, then the other company which is left shall escape.

This news greatly alarmed Jacob, who attempted to create a last-minute diversion for half his company.

And Jacob said, O God of my father Abraham, and God of my father Isaac, the LORD which saidst unto me, Return unto thy country, and to thy kindred, and I will deal well with thee: I am not worthy of the least of all the mercies, and of all the truth, which Thou hast shewed unto Thy servant; for with my staff I passed over this Jordan; and now I am become two bands. Deliver me, I pray Thee, from the hand of my brother, from the hand of Esau: for I fear him, lest he will come and smite me, and the mother with the children. And Thou saidst, I will surely do

thee good, and make thy seed as the sand of the sea, which cannot be numbered for multitude.

Jacob called out to the God who had been with him from the beginning, (Genesis 28:10-15).

And he lodged there that same night; and took of that which came to his hand a present for Esau his brother; two hundred she goats, and twenty he goats, two hundred ewes, and twenty rams, thirty milch camels with their colts, forty kine, and ten bulls, twenty she asses, and ten foals. And he delivered them into the hand of his servants, every drove by themselves; and said unto his servants, Pass over before me, and put a space betwixt drove and drove. And he commanded the foremost, saying, When Esau my brother meeteth thee, and asketh thee, saying, Whose art thou? And whither goest thou? And whose are these before thee? Then thou shalt say, They be thy servant Jacob's; it is a present sent unto my lord Esau: and, behold, also he is behind us. And so commanded he the second, and the third, and all that followed the droves, saying, On this manner shall ye speak unto Esau, when ye find him. And say ye moreover, Behold, thy servant Jacob is behind us. For he said, I will appease him with the present that goeth before me, and afterward I will see his face; peradventure he will accept of me. So went the present over before him:

Jacob hoped to pacify any feelings of resentment Esau might still have had.

and himself lodged that night in the company. And he rose up that night, and took his two wives, and his two womenservants, and his eleven sons, and passed

over the ford Jabbok. And he took them, and sent them over the brook, and sent over that he had.

Jacob tried to put as much distance as possible between Esau and his family incase they should have to escape.

And Jacob was left alone; and there wrestled a Man with him until the breaking of the day.

One from the band of angels Jacob encountered, (Genesis 32:1, 2), confronted him.

And when He saw that He prevailed not against him,

Jacob, who was unaware of who this man was, struggled for his life.

He touched the hollow of his thigh; and the hollow of Jacob's thigh was out of joint, as he wrestled with Him.

The man revealed His super-human power.

And He said, Let Me go, for the day breaketh.

He bid Jacob, who now realized who He was, to let Him go.

And he said, I will not let Thee go, except Thou bless me. And He said unto him, What is thy name? And he said, Jacob. And He said, Thy name shall be called no more Jacob, but Israel: for as a prince hast thou power with God and with men, and hast prevailed.

Upon receiving supplication from Jacob, He richly blessed him. Israel means "The prince of God" in Hebrew!

And Jacob asked Him, and said, Tell me, I pray Thee, Thy Name.

Jacob wanted to make sure the Man was who he thought He was.

And He said, Wherefore is it that thou dost ask after My Name? And He blessed him there.

It was unnecessary for Him to tell Jacob His Name, (Exodus 3:14, 15), in order to bless him.

And Jacob called the name of the place Peniel: For I have seen God face to face, and my life is preserved.

Jacob had just encountered God face-to-face, and knew how unbelievable that was, (Exodus 33:20).

And as he passed over Penuel the sun rose upon him, and he halted upon his thigh. Therefore the children of Israel eat not of the sinew which shrank, which is upon the hollow of the thigh, unto this day: because He touched the hollow of Jacob's thigh in the sinew that shrank.

God had miraculously made the muscle sinews that connect the femur to the coxal bone shrink, (Genesis 32:25)!

Chapter 33

And Jacob lifted up his eyes, and looked, and, behold, Esau came, and with him four hundred men. And he divided the children unto Leah, and unto Rachel, and unto the two handmaids. And he put the handmaids and their children foremost, and Leah and her children after, and Rachel and Joseph hindermost. And he

passed over before them, and bowed himself to the ground seven times, until he came near to his brother.

He did everything he could to protect his wives and children, especially Rachel and Joseph.

And Esau ran to meet him, and embraced him, and fell on his neck, and kissed him: and they wept.

They were moved upon seeing one another again after so long.

And he lifted up his eyes, and saw the women and the children; and said, Who are those with thee?

Esau could not believe how God had blessed Jacob.

And he said, The children which God hath graciously given thy servant.

Jacob honestly told Esau it was God who had so richly blessed him.

Then the handmaidens came near, they and their children, and they bowed themselves. And Leah also with her children came near, and bowed themselves: and after came Joseph near and Rachel, and they bowed themselves.

Jacob's family then proceeded to show Esau they acknowledged their relationship with him, Jacob's brother.

And he said, What meanest thou by all this drove which I met? And he said, These are to find grace in the sight of my lord. And Esau said, I have enough, my brother; keep that thou hast unto thyself.

Esau was content with being reunited with Jacob, and had no desire for gifts.

And Jacob said, Nay, I pray thee, if now I have found grace in thy sight, then receive my present at my hand: for therefore I have seen thy face, as though I had seen the Face of God, and thou wast pleased with me.

Jacob compared his meeting Esau with his meeting God face-to-face the night before, (Genesis 32:24, Genesis 32:30).

Take, I pray thee, my blessing that is brought to thee; because God hath dealt graciously with me, and because I have enough. And he urged him, and he took it.

Jacob wanted to share from out of his abundance with Esau.

And he said, Let us take our journey, and let us go, and I will go before thee.

Esau wanted to provide what he could for his younger brother, (Genesis 25:25).

And he said unto him, My lord knoweth that the children are tender, and the flocks and herds with young are with me: and if men should overdrive them one day, all the flock will die. Let my lord, I pray thee, pass over before his servant: and I will lead on softly, according as the cattle that goeth before me and the children be able to endure, until I come unto my lord unto Seir. And Esau said, Let me now leave with thee some of the folk that are with me. And he said, What needeth it? Let me find grace in the sight of my lord.

Jacob was simply relieved to be safely reconciled with Esau, and saw no further need for protection from anyone or anything.

So Esau returned that day on his way unto Seir.

The brothers parted paths.

And Jacob journeyed to Succoth, and built him an house, and made booths for his cattle: therefore the name of the place is called Succoth.

Jacob could now settle down with his family. No longer fleeing from Esau, (Genesis 27:43), nor from Laban, (Genesis 31:20), he could tend his animals without having to worry about dangerous relatives.

And Jacob came to Shalem, a city of Shechem, which is in the land of Canaan, when he came from Padanaram; and pitched his tent before the city. And he bought a parcel of a field, where he had spread his tent, at the hand of the children of Hamor, Shechem's father, for an hundred pieces of money. And he erected there an altar, and called it Eleloheisrael.

Jacob's relationship with the people of this city quickly became a hostile one, (Genesis 34).

Chapter 34

And Dinah the daughter of Leah, which she bare unto Jacob, went out to see the daughters of the land. And when Shechem the son of Hamor the Hivite, prince of the country, saw her, he took her, and lay with her, and defiled her.

Shechem, prince of where they lived, wronged Jacob's daughter.

And his soul clave unto Dinah the daughter of Jacob, and he loved the damsel, and spake kindly unto the damsel.

His feelings of physical ardor quickly turned to what he thought was love.

And Shechem spake unto his father Hamor, saying, Get me this damsel to wife.

Shechem hoped his father would help him transform his fantasy into a reality.

And Jacob heard that he had defiled Dinah his daughter: now his sons were with his cattle in the field: and Jacob held his peace until they were come.

Jacob was afraid of the reaction he would induce upon telling his sons.

And Hamor the father of Shechem went out unto Jacob to commune with him.

Hamor wanted to rectify his son's actions towards Jacob's daughter.

And the sons of Jacob came out of the field when they heard it: and the men were grieved, and they were very wroth, because he had wrought folly in Israel in lying with Jacob's daughter; which thing ought not to be done.

Once the occurrence became known, there was little Jacob could do to hold back his sons.

And Hamor communed with them, saying, The soul of my son Shechem longeth for your daughter: I pray you give her him to wife. And make ye marriages with us, and give your daughters unto us, and take our daughters unto you. And ye shall dwell with us: and the land shall be before you; dwell and trade ye therein, and get you possessions therein.

Hamor suggested comingling with Jacob's people in order to take care of the issue at hand.

And Shechem said unto her father and unto her brethren, Let me find grace in your eyes, and what ye shall say unto me I will give. Ask me never so much

dowry and gift, and I will give according as ye shall say unto me: but give me the damsel to wife.

So strongly did Shechem desire her, he was willing to do whatever he was requested.

And the sons of Jacob answered Shechem and Hamor his father deceitfully, and said, because he had defiled Dinah their sister: and they said unto them, We cannot do this thing, to give our sister to one that is uncircumcised; for that were a reproach unto us: but in this will we consent unto you: if ye will be as we be, that every male of you be circumcised; then will we give our daughters unto you, and we will take your daughters to us, and we will dwell with you, and we will become one people. But if ye will not hearken unto us, to be circumcised; then will we take our daughter, and we will be gone.

Jacob's sons pretended to be in favor of Hamor's suggestion of comingling. Having Shechem's male subjects experience circumcision played into their tactics, (Genesis 34:25, 26).

And their words pleased Hamor, and Shechem Hamor's son. And the young man deferred not to do the thing, because he had delight in Jacob's daughter: and he was more honourable than all the house of his father.

Shechem unknowingly secured his own death. His want blinded him from the truth.

And Hamor and Shechem his son came unto the gate of their city, and communed with the men of their city, saying, These men are peaceable with us; therefore let them dwell in the land, and trade therein; for the land, behold, it is large enough for them; let us take their daughters to us for wives, and let us give them

our daughters. Only herein will the men consent unto us for to dwell with us, to be one people, if every male among us be circumcised, as they are circumcised. Shall not their cattle and their substance and every beast of theirs be ours? Only let us consent unto them, and they will dwell with us.

They excitedly told the ostensive tidings to the male populace of the city.

And unto Hamor and unto Shechem his son hearkened all that went out of the gate of his city; and every male was circumcised, all that went out of the gate of his city.

They expected Jacob's sons to uphold their side of their unauthentic covenant, (Genesis 34:15, 16).

And it came to pass on the third day, when they were sore, that two of the sons of Jacob, Simeon and Levi, Dinah's brethren, took each man his sword, and came upon the city boldly, and slew all the males. And they slew Hamor and Shechem his son with the edge of the sword, and took Dinah out of Shechem's house, and went out. The sons of Jacob came upon the slain, and spoiled the city, because they had defiled their sister. They took their sheep, and their oxen, and their asses, and that which was in the city, and that which was in the field, and all their wealth, and all their little ones, and their wives took they captive, and spoiled even all that was in the house.

Their cruel acts would take away their father's blessing from them, (Genesis 49:5-7).

And Jacob said to Simeon and Levi, Ye have troubled me to make me to stink among the inhabitants of the land, among the Canaanites and the Perizzites:

and I being few in number, they shall gather themselves together against me, and slay me; and I shall be destroyed, I and my house.

Jacob did not believe they could survive Canaanite retaliation.

And they said, Should he deal with our sister as with an harlot?

Their reply showed him they still had feelings of anger.

Chapter 35

And God said unto Jacob, Arise, go up to Bethel, and dwell there: and make there an altar unto God, that appeared unto thee when thou fleddest from the face of Esau thy brother.

God wanted to remind Jacob of how He had guided each step throughout his past.

Then Jacob said unto his household, and to all that were with him, Put away the strange gods that are among you, and be clean, and change your garments: and let us arise, and go up to Bethel; and I will make there an altar unto God, who answered me in the day of my distress, and was with me in the way which I went.

Jacob was certain that God would show them where they needed to journey.

And they gave unto Jacob all the strange gods which were in their hand, and all their earrings which were in their ears; and Jacob hid them under the oak which was by Shechem.

Jacob expunged all the objects that reminded him of their past, (Genesis 31:19).

And they journeyed: and the terror of God was upon the cities that were round about them, and they did not pursue after the sons of Jacob.

God aided them during their escape supernaturally.

So Jacob came to Luz, which is in the land of Canaan, that is, Bethel, he and all the people that were with him. And he built there an altar, and called the place Elbethel: because there God appeared unto him, when he fled from the face of his brother.

Jacob showed his gratitude upon arriving at their destination by renaming it El-bethel, meaning "the God of Bethel".

But Deborah Rebekah's nurse died, and she was buried beneath Bethel under an oak: and the name of it was called Allonbachuth.

Allonbachuth, or "Oak of weeping", was the name given to where Jacob's mother's handmaiden now rested.

And God appeared unto Jacob again, when he came out of Padanaram, and blessed him. And God said unto him, Thy name is Jacob: thy name shall not be called any more Jacob, but Israel shall be thy name: and He called his name Israel.

God reminded Jacob of his transformation from the supplanter to the prince.

And God said unto him, I am God Almighty: be fruitful and multiply; a nation and a company of nations shall be of thee, and kings shall come out of thy loins; and the land which I gave Abraham and Isaac, to thee I will give it, and to thy seed

after thee will I give the land. And God went up from him in the place where He talked with him.

God reestablished His covenant with him.

And Jacob set up a pillar in the place where He talked with him, even a pillar of stone: and he poured a drink offering thereon, and he poured oil thereon. And Jacob called the name of the place where God spake with him, Bethel.

It was the same place where God originally made a covenant with Jacob, (Genesis 28:13-15).

And they journeyed from Bethel; and there was but a little way to come to Ephrath: and Rachel travailed, and she had hard labour. And it came to pass, when she was in hard labour, that the midwife said unto her, Fear not; thou shalt have this son also.

Rachel's midwife wanted to give her hope that she would make it to their destination without a miscarriage.

And it came to pass, as her soul was in departing, (for she died) that she called his name Benoni: but his father called him Benjamin.

Having realized she was going to die, Rachel named this child Benoni, or "Son of my sorrow". A living memorial of his mother, he was special to Jacob, and so he named him Benjamin, or "Son of my right hand".

And Rachel died, and was buried in the way to Ephrath, which is Bethlehem. And Jacob set a pillar upon her grave: that is the pillar of Rachel's grave unto this day.

Jacob signified the place of Rachel's burial with a permanent expression of his sorrow.

And Israel journeyed, and spread his tent beyond the tower of Edar.

Jacob journeyed on, clinging on to what God had recently promised him, (Genesis 35:11, 12).

And it came to pass, when Israel dwelt in that land, that Reuben went and lay with Bilhah his father's concubine: and Israel heard it.

Leah's first son, Rueben, took advantage of his knowledge of Jacob and his wives' sleeping habits, (Genesis 30:14-16).

Now the sons of Jacob were twelve: the sons of Leah; Reuben, Jacob's firstborn, and Simeon, and Levi, and Judah, and Issachar, and Zebulun: the sons of Rachel; Joseph, and Benjamin: and the sons of Bilhah, Rachel's handmaid; Dan, and Naphtali: and the sons of Zilpah, Leah's handmaid; Gad, and Asher: these are the sons of Jacob, which were born to him in Padanaram.

From these twelve sons would descend the twelve tribes of Israel, (Numbers 1:20-43, 47).

And Jacob came unto Isaac his father unto Mamre, unto the city of Arbah, which is Hebron, where Abraham and Isaac sojourned. And the days of Isaac were an hundred and fourscore years. And Isaac gave up the ghost, and died, and was gathered unto his people, being old and full of days: and his sons Esau and Jacob buried him.

Upon witnessing his father's death, Esau made sure to calm any suspicions that Jacob and his family might have had by joining him in the burial ceremony.

Chapter 36

Now these are the generations of Esau, who is Edom. Esau took his wives of the daughters of Canaan; Adah the daughter of Elon the Hittite, and Aholibamah the daughter of Anah the daughter of Zibeon the Hivite; and Bashemath Ishmael's daughter, sister of Nebajoth.

These women were a source of hardship for Isaac and Rebekah, (Genesis 26:34, 35, Genesis 27:46, Genesis 28:8).

And Adah bare to Esau Eliphaz; and Bashemath bare Reuel; and Aholibamah bare Jeush, and Jaalam, and Korah: these are the sons of Esau, which were born unto him in the land of Canaan.

Esau would continue to benefit from the blessing he was able to procure from Isaac, (Genesis 27:34-38).

And Esau took his wives, and his sons, and his daughters, and all the persons of his house, and his cattle, and all his beasts, and all his substance, which he had got in the land of Canaan; and went into the country from the face of his brother Jacob. For their riches were more than that they might dwell together; and the land wherein they were strangers could not bear them because of their cattle.

Esau realized the blessing Isaac gave Jacob far outweighed the one he received, (Genesis 27:28, 29, Genesis 27:39, 40).

Thus dwelt Esau in mount Seir: Esau is Edom.

The nation of Edom would prove to be a hostile one to the nation of Israel, (Numbers 20:14-21, Judges 11:17, 1 Kings 11:14, Ezekiel 35, Obadiah 1).

And these are the generations of Esau the father of the Edomites in mount Seir: these are the names of Esau's sons; Eliphaz the son of Adah the wife of Esau, Reuel the son of Bashemath the wife of Esau. And the sons of Eliphaz were Teman, Omar, Zepho, and Gatam, and Kenaz. And Timna was concubine to Eliphaz Esau's son; and she bare to Eliphaz Amalek: these were the sons of Adah Esau's wife. And these are the sons of Reuel; Nahath, and Zerah, Shammah, and Mizzah: these were the sons of Bashemath Esau's wife. And these were the sons of Aholibamah, the daughter of Anah the daughter of Zibeon, Esau's wife: and she bare to Esau Jeush, and Jaalam, and Korah. These were dukes of the sons of Esau: the sons of Eliphaz the firstborn son of Esau; duke Teman, duke Omar, duke Zepho, duke Kenaz, duke Korah, duke Gatam, and duke Amalek: these are the dukes that came of Eliphaz in the land of Edom; these were the sons of Adah. And these are the sons of Reuel Esau's son; duke Nahath, duke Zerah, duke Shammah, duke Mizzah: these are the dukes that came of Reuel in the land of Edom; these are the sons of Bashemath Esau's wife. And these are the sons of Aholibamah Esau's wife; duke Jeush, duke Jaalam, duke Korah: these were the dukes that came of Aholibamah the daughter of Anah, Esau's wife. These are the sons of Esau, who is Edom, and these are their dukes.

These descendants of Esau would displace the current inhabitants of Mt Seir, (Genesis 36:20-30).

These are the sons of Seir the Horite, who inhabited the land; Lotan, and Shobal, and Zibeon, and Anah, and Dishon, and Ezer, and Dishan: these are the dukes of the Horites, the children of Seir in the land of Edom. And the children of Lotan were Hori and Hemam; and Lotan's sister was Timna. And the children of Shobal were these; Alvan, and Manahath, and Ebal, Shepho, and Onam. And these are the children of Zibeon; both Ajah, and Anah: this was that Anah that found the mules in the wilderness, as he fed the asses of Zibeon his father. And the children of Anah were these; Dishon, and Aholibamah the daughter of Anah. And these are the children of Dishon; Hemdan, and Eshban, and Ithran, and Cheran. The children of Ezer are these; Bilhan, and Zaavan, and Akan. The children of Dishan are these; Uz, and Aran. These are the dukes that came of the Horites; duke Lotan, duke Shobal, duke Zibeon, duke Anah, duke Dishon, duke Ezer, duke Dishan: these are the dukes that came of Hori, among their dukes in the land of Seir.

These indigenous rulers were no match for Esau's lineage, (Genesis 36:9-19).

And these are the kings that reigned in the land of Edom, before there reigned any king over the children of Israel. And Bela the son of Beor reigned in Edom: and the name of his city was Dinhabah. And Bela died, and Jobab the son of Zerah of Bozrah reigned in his stead. And Jobab died, and Husham of the land of Temani reigned in his stead. And Husham died, and Hadad the son of Bedad, who smote Midian in the field of Moab, reigned in his stead: and the name of his city was Avith. And Hadad died, and Samlah of Masrekah reigned in his stead. And Samlah died, and Saul of Rehoboth by the river reigned in his stead. And Saul died, and Baalhanan the son of Achbor reigned in his stead. And Baalhanan the son of Achbor died, and Hadar reigned in his stead: and the name of his city was Pau; and his wife's name was Mehetabel, the daughter of Matred, the daughter of Mezahab. And these are the names of the dukes that came of Esau, according to their families, after their places, by their names; duke Timnah, duke Alvah, duke Jetheth, duke Aholibamah, duke Elah, duke Pinon, duke Kenaz, duke Teman, duke Mibzar, duke Magdiel, duke Iram: these be the dukes of Edom, according to their habitations in the land of their possession: he is Esau the father of the Edomites.

Esau's posterity would inhabit Mt Seir permanently, (Deuteronomy 2:5).

Chapter 37

And Jacob dwelt in the land wherein his father was a stranger, in the land of Canaan. These are the generations of Jacob. Joseph, being seventeen years old, was feeding the flock with his brethren; and the lad was with the sons of Bilhah, and with the sons of Zilpah, his father's wives:

The menial tasks such as tending sheep were given to Jacob's concubines' sons; Joseph was only there to supervise them.

and Joseph brought unto his father their evil report.

Joseph honestly related what he had seen during his time with his brothers.

Now Israel loved Joseph more than all his children, because he was the son of his old age: and he made him a coat of many colours.

Being the firstborn son of the deceased Rachel, (Genesis 30:22-24), Joseph held a special place in Jacob's heart.

And when his brethren saw that their father loved him more than all his brethren, they hated him, and could not speak peaceably unto him.

Joseph's brothers were jealous of the extravagant love he received from their father.

And Joseph dreamed a dream, and he told it his brethren: and they hated him yet the more. And he said unto them, Hear, I pray you, this dream which I have dreamed: for, behold, we were binding sheaves in the field, and lo, my sheaf arose, and also stood upright; and, behold, your sheaves stood round about, and made obeisance to my sheaf.

God used this dream to tell Joseph how He planned to use him in the future, (Genesis 45:5-7).

And his brethren said to him, Shalt thou indeed reign over us? Or shalt thou indeed have dominion over us? And they hated him yet the more for his dreams, and for his words.

His brothers, who did not fully understand the dream, did not want to believe its apparent meaning.

And he dreamed yet another dream, and told it his brethren, and said, Behold, I have dreamed a dream more; and behold, the sun and the moon and the eleven stars made obeisance to me.

God was showing Joseph the important position he would hold in his family.

And he told it to his father, and to his brethren: and his father rebuked him, and said unto him, What is this dream that thou hast dreamed? Shall I and thy mother and thy brethren indeed come to bow down ourselves to thee to the earth? And his brethren envied him; but his father observed the saying.

Jacob understood it's meaning, but was afraid to tell it to his sons.

And his brethren went to feed their father's flock in Shechem. And Israel said unto Joseph, Do not thy brethren feed the flock in Shechem? Come, and I will send thee unto them. And he said to him, Here am I. And he said to him, Go, I pray thee, see whether it be well with thy brethren, and well with the flocks; and bring me word again. So he sent him out of the vale of Hebron, and he came to Shechem.

Jacob had no idea he would not see his son again for twenty-two years, (Genesis 37:2, Genesis 41:46, Genesis 41:53, Genesis 45:6, Genesis 46:29).

And a certain man found him, and, behold, he was wandering in the field: and the man asked him, saying, What seekest thou? And he said, I seek my brethren: tell me, I pray thee, where they feed their flocks. And the man said, They are departed hence; for I heard them say, Let us go to Dothan. And Joseph went after his brethren, and found them in Dothan.

Joseph was unaware of how his brothers were going to treat him, (Genesis 37:23-28).

And when they saw him afar off, even before he came near unto them, they conspired against him to slay him. And they said one to another, Behold, this dreamer cometh. Come now therefore, and let us slay him, and cast him into

some pit, and we will say, Some evil beast hath devoured him: and we shall see what will become of his dreams.

God's plan for Joseph's life began unfolding.

And Reuben heard it, and he delivered him out of their hands; and said, Let us not kill him. And Reuben said unto them, Shed no blood, but cast him into this pit that is in the wilderness, and lay no hand upon him; that he might rid him out of their hands, to deliver him to his father again.

Reuben remembered how Jacob had made it publicly known how much he loved Joseph, (Genesis 37:3), and was afraid that his brothers' scheme would break his heart.

And it came to pass, when Joseph was come unto his brethren, that they stript Joseph out of his coat, his coat of many colours that was on him; and they took him, and cast him into a pit: and the pit was empty, there was no water in it. And they sat down to eat bread: and they lifted up their eyes and looked, and, behold, a company of Ishmeelites came from Gilead with their camels bearing spicery and balm and myrrh, going to carry it down to Egypt.

The prospect of selling Joseph to this caravan provided a way in which they could get rid of Joseph without having to take responsibility if he were to die.

And Judah said unto his brethren, What profit is it if we slay our brother, and conceal his blood? Come, and let us sell him to the Ishmeelites, and let not our hand be upon him; for he is our brother and our flesh. And his brethren were content.

Speaking out against killing Joseph would bring his father's blessing on him, (Genesis 49:8-12).

Then there passed by Midianites merchantmen; and they drew and lifted up Joseph out of the pit, and sold Joseph to the Ishmeelites for twenty pieces of silver: and they brought Joseph into Egypt.

Joseph would not acquire his freedom for another thirteen years, (Genesis 41:46).

And Reuben returned unto the pit; and, behold, Joseph was not in the pit; and he rent his clothes. And he returned unto his brethren, and said, The child is not; and I, whither shall I go?

Reuben did not want to relate what they had done to Joseph to their father.

And they took Joseph's coat, and killed a kid of the goats, and dipped the coat in the blood; and they sent the coat of many colours, and they brought it to their father; and said, This have we found: know now whether it be thy son's coat or no.

Joseph's brothers were hoping to conceal what they had done.

And he knew it, and said, It is my son's coat; an evil beast hath devoured him; Joseph is without doubt rent in pieces. And Jacob rent his clothes, and put sackcloth upon his loins, and mourned for his son many days. And all his sons and all his daughters rose up to comfort him; but he refused to be comforted; and he said, For I will go down into the grave unto my son mourning. Thus his father wept for him.

Jacob's grief was intense from having lost the firstborn son of his beloved Rachel, (Genesis 30:22-24).

And the Midianites sold him into Egypt unto Potiphar, an officer of Pharaoh's, and captain of the guard.

Joseph's time in Egypt would begin arduously, (Genesis 39:7-20).

Chapter 38

And it came to pass at that time, that Judah went down from his brethren, and turned in to a certain Adullamite, whose name was Hirah. And Judah saw there a daughter of a certain Canaanite, whose name was Shuah; and he took her, and went in unto her. And she conceived, and bare a son; and he called his name Er. And she conceived again, and bare a son; and she called his name Onan.

Onan would cause Er's wife to lose hope of ever having children, (Genesis 38:9).

And she yet again conceived, and bare a son; and called his name Shelah: and he was at Chezib, when she bare him. And Judah took a wife for Er his firstborn, whose name was Tamar.

Tamar would have to trick Judah into giving her children, (Genesis 38:14-26).

And Er, Judah's firstborn, was wicked in the sight of the LORD; and the LORD slew him.

Tamar was left without a husband.

And Judah said unto Onan, Go in unto thy brother's wife, and marry her, and raise up seed to thy brother. And Onan knew that the seed should not be his; and

it came to pass, when he went in unto his brother's wife, that he spilled it on the ground, lest that he should give seed to his brother.

Onan's wicked deed would cause his brother's name to disappear from existence.

And the thing which he did displeased the LORD: wherefore He slew him also.

Tamar was now widowed for the second time.

Then said Judah to Tamar his daughter in law, Remain a widow at thy father's house, till Shelah my son be grown: for he said, Lest peradventure he die also, as his brethren did. And Tamar went and dwelt in her father's house.

Tamar obeyed Judah, trusting that he would keep his word.

And in process of time the daughter of Shuah Judah's wife died; and Judah was comforted, and went up unto his sheepshearers to Timnath, he and his friend Hirah the Adullamite. And it was told Tamar, saying, Behold thy father in law goeth up to Timnath to shear his sheep.

Tamar saw how Judah could quickly forget about his female children.

And she put her widow's garments off from her, and covered her with a veil, and wrapped herself, and sat in an open place, which is by the way to Timnath; for she saw that Shelah was grown, and she was not given unto him to wife.

Judah had not kept his word, (Genesis 38:11).

When Judah saw her, he thought her to be an harlot; because she had covered her face. And he turned unto her by the way, and said, Go to, I pray thee, let me come in unto thee; (for he knew not that she was his daughter in law).

Judah believed his choice would go undiscovered.

And she said, What wilt thou give me, that thou mayest come in unto me? And he said, I will send thee a kid from the flock. And she said, Wilt thou give me a pledge, till thou send it?

She was sure to provide for proof of his father-ship of her children, (Genesis 38:26).

And he said, What pledge shall I give thee? And she said, Thy signet, and thy bracelets, and thy staff that is in thine hand.

These items would be unmistakable to identify.

And he gave it her, and came in unto her, and she conceived by him. And she arose, and went away, and laid by her veil from her, and put on the garments of her widowhood.

Her disguise went undetected by Judah.

And Judah sent the kid by the hand of his friend the Adullamite, to receive his pledge from the woman's hand: but he found her not.

Judah was embarrassed to be seen talking with her.

Then he asked the men of that place, saying, Where is the harlot, that was openly by the way side? And they said, There was no harlot in this place.

Tamar had made sure to return as soon as possible.

And he returned to Judah, and said, I cannot find her; and also the men of the place said, There was no harlot in this place. And Judah said, Let her take it to her, lest we be shamed: behold, I sent this kid, and thou hast not found her.

Judah did not want to draw extra attention to his situation.

And it came to pass about three months after, that it was told Judah, saying, Tamar thy daughter in law hath played the harlot; and also, behold, she is with child by whoredom.

Tamar could not hide her pregnancy any longer.

And Judah said, Bring her forth, and let her be burnt.

Judah did not know he would be killing his own children.

When she was brought forth, she sent to her father in law, saying, By the man, whose these are, am I with child:

Tamar needed to reveal the truth in order to live.

and she said, Discern, I pray thee, whose are these, the signet, and bracelets, and staff.

Tamar had the power to shame him openly.

And Judah acknowledged them, and said, She hath been more righteous than I; because that I gave her not to Shelah my son.

Judah realized how he had disappointed his daughter-in-law by not keeping his word, (Genesis 38:11).

And he knew her again no more.

There would be no reason to accuse her hereafter of committing the crime she had been forced to commit.

And it came to pass in the time of her travail, that, behold, twins were in her womb. And it came to pass, when she travailed, that the one put out his hand: and the midwife took and bound upon his hand a scarlet thread, saying, This came out first.

Tamar's first child was supposed to be the one whom the birthright was passed on to.

And it came to pass, as he drew back his hand, that, behold, his brother came out: and she said, How hast thou broken forth? This breach be upon thee: therefore his name was called Pharez. And afterward came out his brother, that had the scarlet thread upon his hand: and his name was called Zarah.

It was her second son through whom Jesus Christ would descend, (Matthew 1:1-3).

Chapter 39

And Joseph was brought down to Egypt; and Potiphar, an officer of Pharaoh, captain of the guard, an Egyptian, bought him of the hands of the Ishmeelites, which had brought him down thither. And the LORD was with Joseph, and he was a prosperous man; and he was in the house of his master the Egyptian.

Potiphar was happy to have such a dutiful slave.

And his master saw that the LORD was with him, and that the LORD made all that he did to prosper in his hand.

Joseph's talent as a worker was soon recognized by Potiphar.

And Joseph found grace in his sight, and he served him: and he made him overseer over his house, and all that he had he put into his hand. And it came to pass from the time that he had made him overseer in his house, and over all that he had, that the LORD blessed the Egyptian's house for Joseph's sake; and the blessing of the LORD was upon all that he had in the house, and in the field.

God was helping Joseph to achieve his destiny, (Genesis 37:7).

And he left all that he had in Joseph's hand; and he knew not ought he had, save the bread which he did eat. And Joseph was a goodly person, and well favoured. And it came to pass after these things, that his master's wife cast her eyes upon Joseph;

Joseph had gained Potiphar's total trust, who was unsuspecting of his wife's growing infatuation with Joseph.

and she said, Lie with me. But he refused, and said unto his master's wife, Behold, my master wotteth not what is with me in the house, and he hath committed all that he hath to my hand; there is none greater in this house than I; neither hath he kept back any thing from me but thee, because thou art his wife:

Joseph understood this would cause Potiphar immense pain.

how then can I do this great wickedness, and sin against God?

Potiphar's wife did not understand how wicked this was.

And it came to pass, as she spake to Joseph day by day, that he hearkened not unto her, to lie by her, or to be with her. And it came to pass about this time, that

Joseph went into the house to do his business; and there was none of the men of the house there within. And she caught him by his garment, saying, Lie with me:

She had given in and no longer cared about her husband.

and he left his garment in her hand, and fled, and got him out.

Hurting Potiphar was the last thing that Joseph wanted to do.

And it came to pass, when she saw that he had left his garment in her hand, and was fled forth, that she called unto the men of her house, and spake unto them, saying, See, he hath brought in an Hebrew unto us to mock us; he came in unto me to lie with me, and I cried with a loud voice: and it came to pass, when he heard that I lifted up my voice and cried, that he left his garment with me, and fled, and got him out.

Potiphar's wife knew how her husband would take it if he found out that she had approached Joseph.

And she laid up his garment by her, until his lord came home.

She intended to provide as much proof as possible to support the false story she had improvised, (Genesis 39:13-15).

And she spake unto him according to these words, saying, The Hebrew servant, which thou hast brought unto us, came in unto me to mock me: and it came to pass, as I lifted up my voice and cried, that he left his garment with me, and fled out. And it came to pass, when his master heard the words of his wife, which she spake unto him, saying, After this manner did thy servant to me; that his wrath was kindled.

Joseph's master did not know whether or not to play along with his wife's story.

And Joseph's master took him, and put him into the prison, a place where the king's prisoners were bound: and he was there in the prison.

Potiphar knew Joseph would never abuse his trust, and could not let him be executed.

But the LORD was with Joseph, and shewed him mercy, and gave him favour in the sight of the keeper of the prison.

God continued to help Joseph and made it possible for him to gain the prison keeper's trust.

And the keeper of the prison committed to Joseph's hand all the prisoners that were in the prison; and whatsoever they did there, he was the doer of it.

Over time, Joseph inherited the responsibilities the prison keeper.

The keeper of the prison looked not to any thing that was under his hand; because the LORD was with him, and that which he did, the LORD made it to prosper.

God was preparing a plan with which Joseph could be released from prison, (Genesis 40:3, 4).

Chapter 40

And it came to pass after these things, that the butler of the king of Egypt and his baker had offended their lord the king of Egypt. And Pharaoh was wroth against

two of his officers, against the chief of the butlers, and against the chief of the bakers.

These men would be used by God in designing Joseph's release from prison, (Genesis 41:9-13).

And he put them in ward in the house of the captain of the guard, into the prison, the place where Joseph was bound. And the captain of the guard charged Joseph with them, and he served them: and they continued a season in ward.

Joseph was still under Potiphar's command, (Genesis 39:1).

And they dreamed a dream both of them, each man his dream in one night, each man according to the interpretation of his dream, the butler and the baker of the king of Egypt, which were bound in the prison.

God was using these dreams by enabling them future insight, (Genesis 41:10-13).

And Joseph came in unto them in the morning, and looked upon them, and, behold, they were sad. And he asked Pharaoh's officers that were with him in the ward of his lord's house, saying, Wherefore look ye so sadly today?

Their expressions told Joseph the anxiety and confusion they were feeling, and he desired to alleviate their suffering. Joseph understood their emotional turmoil, and he wanted to do what he could to help.

And they said unto him, We have dreamed a dream, and there is no interpreter of it. And Joseph said unto them, Do not interpretations belong to God? Tell me them, I pray you.

Joseph knew how to interpret dreams. He was able to correlate images in the dreams with their associated meanings.

And the chief butler told his dream to Joseph, and said to him, In my dream, behold, a vine was before me; and in the vine were three branches: and it was as though it budded, and her blossoms shot forth; and the clusters thereof brought forth ripe grapes: and Pharaoh's cup was in my hand: and I took the grapes, and pressed them into Pharaoh's cup, and I gave the cup into Pharaoh's hand.

Each depiction in the dream represented a different truth about the chief butler's future.

And Joseph said unto him, This is the interpretation of it: the three branches are three days: yet within three days shall Pharaoh lift up thine head, and restore thee unto thy place: and thou shalt deliver Pharaoh's cup into his hand, after the former manner when thou wast his butler.

Joseph revealed to him his destiny.

But think on me when it shall be well with thee, and shew kindness, I pray thee, unto me, and make mention of me unto Pharaoh, and bring me out of this house: for indeed I was stolen away out of the land of the Hebrews: and here also have I done nothing that they should put me into the dungeon.

Joseph provided for a way by which he could be released from prison, (Genesis 41:9-14).

When the chief baker saw that the interpretation was good, he said unto Joseph, I also was in my dream, and behold, I had three white baskets on my head: and in the uppermost basket there was all manner of baked meats for Pharaoh; and the birds did eat them out of the basket upon my head.

The chief baker's dream was brutally honest.

And Joseph answered and said, This is the interpretation thereof: the three baskets are three days: yet within three days shall Pharaoh lift up thy head from off thee, and shall hang thee on a tree; and the birds shall eat thy flesh from off thee.

Joseph did not hesitate to warn him of his fate.

And it came to pass the third day, which was Pharaoh's birthday, that he made a feast unto all his servants: and he lifted up the head of the chief butler and of the chief baker among his servants. And he restored the chief butler unto his butlership again; and he gave the cup into Pharaoh's hand: but he hanged the chief baker: as Joseph had interpreted to them.

What Joseph had interpreted became a reality.

Yet did not the chief butler remember Joseph, but forgat him.

Joseph would be left in prison for two more years, (Genesis 41:1).

Chapter 41

And it came to pass at the end of two full years, that Pharaoh dreamed: and behold, he stood by the river. And behold, there came up out of the river seven well favoured kine and fatfleshed; and they fed in a meadow. And, behold, seven other kine came up after them out of the river, ill favoured and leanfleshed; and stood by the other kine upon the brink of the river. And the ill favoured and leanfleshed kine did eat up the seven well favoured and fat kine. So Pharaoh awoke.

These dreams were given to Pharaoh in order to warn him of the coming famine!

And he slept and dreamed the second time: and behold, seven ears of corn came up upon one stalk, rank and good. And, behold, seven thin ears and blasted with the east wind sprung up after them. And the seven thin ears devoured the seven rank and full ears. And Pharaoh awoke, and, behold, it was a dream.

The purpose of sending him a double dream was to help him understand how urgent the situation was.

And it came to pass in the morning that his spirit was troubled;

Pharaoh knew he had witnessed something of great gravity.

and he sent and called for all the magicians of Egypt, and all the wise men thereof: and Pharaoh told them his dream; but there was none that could interpret them unto Pharaoh.

These men were not in touch with the God who had sent these dreams to Pharaoh.

Then spake the chief butler unto Pharaoh, saying, I do remember my faults this day: Pharaoh was wroth with his servants, and put me in ward in the captain of the guard's house, both me and the chief baker: and we dreamed a dream in one night, I and he; we dreamed each man according to the interpretation of his dream. And there was there with us a young man, an Hebrew, servant to the captain of the guard; and we told him, and he interpreted to us our dreams; to each man according to his dream he did interpret. And it came to pass, as he interpreted to us, so it was; me he restored unto mine office, and him he hanged.

This servant recalled the uncanny accuracy with which Joseph interpreted their dreams.

Then Pharaoh sent and called Joseph, and they brought him hastily out of the dungeon:

Pharaoh had been told of the power of the Hebrews' God, (Genesis 12:17), and he believed everything his servant relayed to him.

and he shaved himself, and changed his raiment, and came in unto Pharaoh.

Joseph saw God's Hand working.

And Pharaoh said unto Joseph, I have dreamed a dream, and there is none that can interpret it: and I have heard say of thee, that thou canst understand a dream to interpret it.

Pharaoh beseeched Joseph to explain the meaning of his dreams.

And Joseph answered Pharaoh, saying, It is not in me: God shall give Pharaoh an answer of peace.

Joseph let Pharaoh know that God sent him those dreams for a reason, and that He would not fail to reveal their message.

And Pharaoh said unto Joseph, In my dream, behold, I stood upon the bank of the river: and, behold, there came up out of the river seven kine, fatfleshed and well favoured; and they fed in a meadow: and behold, seven other kine came up after them, poor and very ill favoured and leanfleshed, such as I never saw in all the land of Egypt for badness: and the lean and the ill favoured kine did eat up

the first seven fat kine: and when they had eaten them up, it could not be known that they had eaten them; but they were still ill favoured, as at the beginning. So I awoke. And I saw in my dream, and, behold, seven ears came up in one stalk, full and good: and behold, seven ears, withered, thin, and blasted with the east wind, sprung up after them: and the thin ears devoured the seven good ears: and I told this unto the magicians; but there was none that could declare it to me.

Pharaoh eagerly waited for Joseph's response.

And Joseph said unto Pharaoh, The dream of Pharaoh is one: God hath shewed Pharaoh what He is about to do. The seven good kine are seven years; and the seven good ears are seven years: the dream is one.

Joseph immediately understood that this was a double dream.

And the seven thin and ill favoured kine that came up after them are seven years; and the seven empty ears blasted with the east wind shall be seven years of famine.

He then proceeded to relay to Pharaoh each symbol's meaning.

This is the thing which I have spoken unto Pharaoh: what God is about to do He sheweth unto Pharaoh. Behold, there come seven years of great plenty throughout all the land of Egypt: and there shall arise after them seven years of famine; and all the plenty shall be forgotten in the land of Egypt; and the famine shall consume the land; and the plenty shall not be known in the land by reason of that famine following; for it shall be very grievous.

Joseph warned Pharaoh of the crisis that was imminent.

And for that the dream was doubled unto Pharaoh twice; it is because the thing is established by God, and God will shortly bring it to pass.

Joseph also explained the urgency with which God was trying to get through to Pharaoh.

Now therefore let Pharaoh look out a man discreet and wise, and set him over the land of Egypt. Let Pharaoh do this, and let him appoint officers over the land, and take up the fifth part of the land of Egypt in the seven plenteous years. And let them gather all the food of those good years that come, and lay up corn under the hand of Pharaoh, and let them keep food in the cities.

Joseph proposed a plan which would guarantee their survival during the famine.

And that food shall be for store to the land against the seven years of famine, which shall be in the land of Egypt, that the land perish not through the famine. And the thing was good in the eyes of Pharaoh, and in the eyes of all his servants.

Everyone present saw the wisdom of Joseph's words.

And Pharaoh said unto his servants, Can we find such a one as this is, a man in whom the Spirit of God is?

Pharaoh recognized a providential Heart working through Joseph.

And Pharaoh said unto Joseph, Forasmuch as God hath shewed thee all this, there is none so discreet and wise as thou art: thou shalt be over my house, and according unto thy word shall all my people be ruled: only in the throne will I be greater than thou.

In raising Joseph to preside over the nation, Pharaoh was allowing God to work through Joseph and benefit Egypt as much as possible.

And Pharaoh said unto Joseph, See, I have set thee over all the land of Egypt. And Pharaoh took off his ring from his hand, and put it upon Joseph's hand, and arrayed him in vestures of fine linen, and put a gold chain about his neck; and he made him to ride in the second chariot which he had; and they cried before him, Bow the knee: and he made him ruler over all the land of Egypt.

Pharaoh's gifts to Joseph designated him as the second most powerful man in his kingdom.

And Pharaoh said unto Joseph, I am Pharaoh, and without thee shall no man lift up his hand or foot in all the land of Egypt.

Joseph was given complete authority to do what he thought was best for the nation of Egypt.

And Pharaoh called Joseph's name Zaphnathpaaneah; and he gave him to wife Asenath the daughter of Potipherah priest of On. And Joseph went out over all the land of Egypt.

Joseph was now officially a member of Egyptian nobility.

And Joseph was thirty years old when he stood before Pharaoh king of Egypt. And Joseph went out from the presence of Pharaoh, and went throughout all the land of Egypt.

Thirteen long years had passed since Joseph's betrayal by his brothers, (Genesis 37:2, 28).

And in the seven plenteous years the earth brought forth by handfuls.

Pharaoh's dream began unfolding exactly as Joseph had interpreted, (Genesis 41:26).

And he gathered up all the food of the seven years, which were in the land of Egypt, and laid up the food in the cities: the food of the field, which was round about every city, laid he up in the same.

Joseph began carrying out the plan he had proposed in front of Pharaoh, (Genesis 41:33-35).

And Joseph gathered corn as the sand of the sea, very much, until he left numbering; for it was without number.

Joseph wanted to make sure there would be enough food to last the entire famine.

And unto Joseph were born two sons before the years of famine came, which Asenath the daughter of Potipherah priest of On bare unto him. And Joseph called the name of the firstborn Manasseh: For God, said he, hath made me forget all my toil, and all my father's house.

The birth of his first son was a milestone for Joseph. God had not only given him his freedom back, but had also enabled him to start over after having lost everything.

And the name of the second called he Ephraim: For God hath caused me to be fruitful in the land of my affliction.

His newly formed family gave him comfort during his time away from his birth family, (Genesis 37:3).

And the seven years of plenteousness, that was in the land of Egypt, were ended.

The second halves of Pharaoh's dream, (Genesis 41:19, 23, 27), began unfolding.

And the seven years of dearth began to come, according as Joseph had said: and the dearth was in all lands; but in all the land of Egypt there was bread.

Joseph's ruler-ship over Egypt enabled them to survive the famine.

And when all the land of Egypt was famished, the people cried to Pharaoh for bread: and Pharaoh said unto all the Egyptians, Go unto Joseph; what he saith to you, do.

Joseph now had Pharaoh's complete trust, as he had Potiphar's and the prison keeper's before, (Genesis 39:4, Genesis 39:22).

And the famine was over all the face of the earth: and Joseph opened all the storehouses, and sold unto the Egyptians; and the famine waxed sore in the land of Egypt. And all countries came into Egypt to Joseph for to buy corn; because that the famine was so sore in all lands.

Joseph was now the second most powerful person in the world.

Chapter 42

Now when Jacob saw that there was corn in Egypt, Jacob said unto his sons, Why do ye look one upon another? And he said, Behold, I have heard that there is corn in Egypt: get you down thither, and buy for us from thence; that we may live, and not die.

The reunion between Joseph and his family would soon come about, (Genesis 45:3-5, Genesis 46:29).

And Joseph's ten brethren went down to buy corn in Egypt.

Joseph's brothers were unaware the surprise they would encounter upon reaching Egypt.

But Benjamin, Joseph's brother, Jacob sent not with his brethren; for he said, Lest peradventure mischief befall him.

Having already lost his favorite son, losing the only remaining son of Rachel, (Genesis 35:24), would have been more than he could bear.

And the sons of Israel came to buy corn among those that came: for the famine was in the land of Canaan. And Joseph was governor over the land, and he it was that sold to all the people of the land: and Joseph's brethren came, and bowed down themselves before him with their faces to the earth.

Joseph's first dream, (Genesis 37:5-7), was being fulfilled literally as well as symbolically!

And Joseph saw his brethren, and he knew them, but made himself strange unto them, and spake roughly unto them; and he said unto them, Whence come ye? And they said, From the land of Canaan to buy food.

Joseph began seeking information on his beloved father, (Genesis 37:3).

And Joseph knew his brethren, but they knew not him. And Joseph remembered the dreams which he dreamed of them, and said unto them, Ye are spies; to see the nakedness of the land ye are come.

Joseph began seeing again God's Hand at work, (Genesis 41:14), and initiated a plan to reunite him to his family.

And they said unto him, Nay, my lord, but to buy food are thy servants come. We are all one man's sons; we are true men, thy servants are no spies.

His brothers were unaware they were a part of God's plan.

And he said unto them, Nay, but to see the nakedness of the land ye are come.

Joseph wanted to test his brothers' characters. Their response would let Joseph know how they had changed since the last time he saw them, (Genesis 37:28).

And they said, Thy servants are twelve brethren, the sons of one man in the land of Canaan; and, behold, the youngest is this day with our father, and one is not.

Their mention of Joseph showed they had remorse over selling him into slavery.

And Joseph said unto them, That is it that I spake unto you, saying, Ye are spies: hereby ye shall be proved: by the life of Pharaoh ye shall not go forth hence, except your youngest brother come hither. Send one of you, and let him fetch your brother, and ye shall be kept in prison, that your words may be proved, whether there be any truth in you: or else by the life of Pharaoh surely ye are spies.

Joseph longed to see his younger brother, Benjamin.

And he put them all together into ward three days.

Joseph wanted to see his brothers' reaction to the suggestion of bringing Benjamin to Egypt in order to prove their honesty. Their reaction would tell Joseph about the condition of their father, Jacob.

And Joseph said unto them the third day, This do, and live; for I fear God: if ye be true men, let one of your brethren be bound in the house of your prison: go ye, carry corn for the famine of your houses: but bring your youngest brother unto me; so shall your words be verified, and ye shall not die.

Having assessed from their reaction that his father's condition was stable enough to send his youngest son to Egypt, Joseph could now request an audience with Benjamin.

And they did so. And they said one to another, We are verily guilty concerning our brother, in that we saw the anguish of his soul, when he besought us, and we would not hear; therefore is this distress come upon us. And Rueben answered them, saying, Spake I not unto you, saying, Do not sin against the child; and ye would not hear? Therefore, behold, also his blood is required.

Their attributing their apparent dilemma to their past sin of selling Joseph into slavery showed all the more their intense remorse.

And they knew not that Joseph understood them; for he spake unto them by an interpreter. And he turned himself about from them, and wept; and returned to them again, and communed with them, and took from them Simeon, and bound him before their eyes.

Joseph was incredibly moved at their obvious change of heart.

Genesis God Cares

Then Joseph commanded to fill their sacks with corn, and to restore every man's money into his sack, and to give them provision for the way: and thus did he unto them.

Although they didn't yet realize it, Joseph's family would never have to worry about having enough money again.

And they laded their asses with the corn, and departed thence. And as one of them opened his sack to give his ass provender in the inn, he espied his money; for, behold, it was in his sack's mouth.

This practical joke by Joseph did not have the effect it was intended to, (Genesis 42:28).

And he said unto his brethren, My money is restored; and, lo, it is even in my sack: and their heart failed them, and they were afraid, saying one to another, What is this that God hath done unto us?

Joseph's brothers perceived this as simply more punishment for having sold Joseph into slavery.

And they came unto Jacob their father unto the land of Canaan, and told him all that befell unto them; saying, The man, who is the lord of the land, spake roughly to us, and took us for spies of the country. And we said unto him, We are true men; we are no spies: we be twelve brethren, sons of our father; one is not, and the youngest is this day with our father in the land of Canaan. And the man, the lord of the country, said unto us, Hereby shall I know that ye are true men; leave one of your brethren here with me, and take food for the famine of your households, and be gone: and bring your youngest brother unto me: then

shall I know that ye are no spies, but that ye are true men: so will I deliver you your brother, and ye shall traffick in the land.

Joseph's brothers tearfully relayed what had happened to them to Jacob.

And it came to pass, as they emptied their sacks, that, behold, every man's bundle of money was in his sack: and when both they and their father saw the bundles of money, they were afraid.

With Simeon still in captivity, (Genesis 42:24), theft was one crime they could not afford to be convicted of.

And Jacob their father said unto them, Me have ye bereaved of my children: Joseph is not, and Simeon is not, and ye will take Benjamin away: all these things are against me.

Jacob had always blamed his older sons for what he thought had happened to Joseph, (Genesis 37:33-35).

And Rueben spake unto his father, saying, Slay my two sons, if I bring him not to thee: deliver him into my hand, and I will bring him to thee again.

Rueben felt partially responsible for not having saved Joseph, (Genesis 37:22, 29).

And he said, My son shall not go down with you; for his brother is dead, and he is left alone: if mischief befall him by the way in the which ye go, then shall ye bring down my gray hairs with sorrow to the grave.

Jacob truly would not have been able to bear the loss of Benjamin.

Chapter 43

And the famine was sore in the land. And it came to pass, when they had eaten up the corn which they had brought out of Egypt, their father said unto them, Go again, buy us a little food.

Jacob now had no choice but to let Benjamin go to Egypt.

And Judah spake unto him, saying, The man did solemnly protest unto us, saying, Ye shall not see my face, except your brother be with you. If thou wilt send our brother with us, we will go down and buy thee food: but if thou wilt not send him, we will not go down: for the man said unto us, Ye shall not see my face, except your brother be with you.

Judah knew that returning to Egypt without Benjamin could result in their permanent detainment, (Genesis 42:15, 16).

And Israel said, Wherefore dealt ye so ill with me, as to tell the man whether ye had yet a brother?

Jacob had not witnessed Joseph interrogate his sons, and was unaware of Joseph's plan to reunite their family.

And they said, The man asked us straitly of our state, and of our kindred, saying, Is your father yet alive? Have ye another brother? And we told him according to the tenor of these words: could we certainly know that he would say, Bring your brother down?

Jacob's sons confessed their powerlessness to predict Joseph's actions.

And Judah said unto Israel his father, Send the lad with me, and we will arise and go; that we may live, and not die, both we, and thou, and also our little ones.

Judah was appealing to Jacob's humanity.

I will be surety for him; of my hand shalt thou require him: if I bring him not unto thee, and set him before thee, then let me bear the blame forever: for except we had lingered, surely now we had returned this second time.

Judah's exhibition of responsibility and leadership here would cause him to receive his father's most excellent blessing, (Genesis 49:8-12).

And their father Israel said unto them, If it must be so now, do this; take of the best fruits in the land in your vessels, and carry down the man a present, a little balm, and a little honey, spices, and myrrh, nuts, and almonds: and take double money in your hand; and the money that was brought again in the mouth of your sacks, carry it again in your hand; peradventure it was an oversight: take also your brother, and arise, go again unto the man: and God Almighty give you mercy before the man, that he may send away your other brother, and Benjamin. If I be bereaved of my children, I am bereaved.

Jacob decided to put his trust in the God who had brought him safely thus far.

And the men took that present, and they took double money in their hand, and Benjamin; and rose up, and went down to Egypt, and stood before Joseph.

Jacob's sons looked forward to clearing their name.

And when Joseph saw Benjamin with them, he said to the ruler of his house, Bring these men home, and slay, and make ready; for these men shall dine with me at noon.

Joseph was preparing to reveal himself to them, (Genesis 45:1-4).

And the man did as Joseph bade; and the man brought the men into Joseph's house. And the men were sore afraid, because they were brought into Joseph's house; and they said, Because of the money that was returned in our sacks at the first time are we brought in; that he may seek occasion against us, and fall upon us, and take us for bondmen, and our asses.

Joseph's brothers were certain they had made this journey in vain.

And they came near to the steward of Joseph's house, and they communed with him at the door of the house, and said, O sir, we came indeed down at the first time to buy food: and it came to pass, when we came to the inn, that we opened our sacks, and, behold, every man's money was in the mouth of his sack, our money in full weight: and we have brought it again in our hand. And other money have we brought down in our hands to buy food: we cannot tell who put our money in our sacks.

They hoped to appease Joseph's supposed wrath.

And he said, Peace be to you, fear not: your God, and the God of your father, hath given you treasure in your sacks: I had your money.

Joseph's servant knew who these men were, and was in on Joseph's plan.

And he brought Simeon out unto them.

Seeing their brother filled them with relief.

And the man brought the men into Joseph's house, and gave them water, and they washed their feet; and he gave their asses provender.

The hospitality shown to them soothed their anxiety.

And they made ready the present against Joseph came at noon: for they heard that they should eat bread there.

Joseph's brothers had not expected to eat lunch with this powerful Egyptian ruler.

And when Joseph came home, they brought him the present which was in their hand into the house, and bowed themselves to him to the earth. And he asked them of their welfare, and said, Is your father well, the old man of whom ye spake? Is he yet alive?

The gifts from his native land filled Joseph with memories, (Genesis 43:11), and he again inquired of his father's wellbeing.

And they answered, Thy servant our father is in good health, he is yet alive. And they bowed down their heads, and made obeisance.

Joseph's brothers were grateful for his good will towards them.

And he lifted up his eyes, and saw his brother Benjamin, his mother's son, and said, Is this your younger brother, of whom ye spake unto me? And he said, God be gracious unto thee, my son. And Joseph made haste; for his bowels did yearn upon his brother: and he sought where to weep; and he entered into his chamber, and wept there.

Seeing the resemblance of his mother moved Joseph to tears.

And he washed his face, and went out, and refrained himself, and said, Set on bread. And they set on for him by himself, and for them by themselves, and for the Egyptians, which did eat with him, by themselves: because the Egyptians might not eat bread with the Hebrews; for that is an abomination unto the Egyptians.

Joseph still wanted to maintain his image as an Egyptian aristocrat in order to give them one final test, (Genesis 44).

And they sat before him, the firstborn according to his birthright, and the youngest according to his youth: and the men marvelled one at another. And he took and sent messes unto them from before him: but Benjamin's mess was five times so much as any of theirs. And they drank, and were merry with him.

This practical joke produced its desired effect.

Chapter 44

And he commanded the steward of his house, saying, Fill the men's sacks with food, as much as they can carry, and put every man's money in his sack's mouth. And put my cup, the silver cup, in the sack's mouth of the youngest, and his corn money.

Joseph was ecstatic to be giving this treasure to his younger brother, (Genesis 43:29).

And he did according to the word that Joseph had spoken. As soon as the morning was light, the men were went away, they and their asses. And when they were

gone out of the city, and not yet far off, Joseph said unto his steward, Up, follow after the men; and when thou dost overtake them, say unto them, Wherefore have ye rewarded evil for good? Is not this it in which my lord drinketh, and whereby indeed he divineth? Ye have done evil in so doing. And he overtook them, and he spake unto them these same words.

Joseph's servant continued to participate in Joseph's plan.

And they said unto him, Wherefore saith my lord these words? God forbid that thy servants should do according to this thing: behold, the money, which we found in our sacks' mouths, we brought again unto thee out of the land of Canaan: how then should we steal out of thy lord's house silver or gold? With whomsoever of thy servants it be found, both let him die, and we also will be my lord's bondmen.

Joseph's brothers were confident in their integrity, as well as the integrity of those with them.

And he said, Now also let it be according unto your words: he with whom it is found shall be my servant; and ye shall be blameless. Then they speedily took down every man his sack to the ground, and opened every man his sack. And he searched, and began at the eldest, and left at the youngest: and the cup was found in Benjamin's sack. Then they rent their clothes, and laded every man his ass, and returned to the city.

They had not expected to be set up two times in a row.

And Judah and his brethren came to Joseph's house; for he was yet there: and they fell before him on the ground.

They were now at Joseph's mercy.

And Joseph said unto them, What deed is this that ye have done? Wot ye not that such a man as I can certainly divine?

Joseph continued to keep up his image.

And Judah said, What shall we say unto my lord? What shall we speak? Or how shall we clear ourselves? God hath found out the iniquity of thy servants: behold, we are my lord's servants, both we, and he also with whom the cup is found.

Joseph's brothers fully believed that God was punishing them for their crime of selling Joseph into slavery.

And he said, God forbid that I should do so: but the man in whose hand the cup is found, he shall be my servant; and as for you, get you up in peace unto your father.

Joseph wanted to test how far they would go to prevent their father's grief.

Then Judah came near unto him, and said, Oh my lord, let thy servant, I pray thee, speak a word in my lord's ears, and let not thine anger burn against thy servant: for thou art even as Pharaoh.

Judah's political adeptness allowed him to speak peacefully with Joseph.

My lord asked his servants, saying, Have ye a father, or a brother? And we said unto my lord, We have a father, an old man, and a child of his old age, a little one;

and his brother is dead, and he alone is left of his mother, and his father loveth him. And thou saidst unto thy servants, Bring him down unto me, that I may set mine eyes upon him. And we said unto my lord, The lad cannot leave his father: for if he should leave his father, his father would die. And thou saidst unto thy servants, Except your youngest bother come down with you, ye shall see my face no more. And it came to pass, when we came up unto thy servant my father, we told him the words of my lord. And our father said, Go again, and buy us a little food. And we said, We cannot go down: if our youngest brother be with us, then will we go down: for we may not see the man's face, except our youngest brother be with us. And thy servant my father said unto us, Ye know that my wife bare me two sons: and the one went out from me, and I said, Surely he is torn in pieces; and I saw him not since: and if ye take this also from me, and mischief befall him, ye shall bring down my gray hairs with sorrow to the grave. For thy servant became surety for the lad unto my father, saying, If I bring him not unto thee, then I shall bear the blame to my father forever. Now therefore, I pray thee, let thy servant abide instead of the lad a bondman to my lord; and let the lad go up with his brethren. For how shall I go up to my father, and the lad be not with me? Lest peradventure I see the evil that shall come on my father.

Judah made a last attempt to dissuade Joseph from holding Benjamin prisoner.

Chapter 45

Then Joseph could not refrain himself before all them that stood by him; and he cried, Cause every man to go out from me. And there stood no man with him,

while Joseph made himself known unto his brethren. And he wept aloud: and the Egyptians and the house of Pharaoh heard.

Judah's heart-felt plea for Jacob and Benjamin was more than Joseph could bear, and he could no longer keep his tears from flowing.

And Joseph said unto his brethren, I am Joseph; doth my father yet live?

Joseph could no longer hold back his eagerness to see his father.

And his brethren could not answer him; for they were troubled at his presence.

Joseph's brothers could not believe how much God had blessed Joseph.

And Joseph said unto his brethren, Come near to me, I pray you. And they came near. And he said, I am Joseph your brother, whom ye sold into Egypt. Now therefore be not grieved, nor angry with yourselves, that ye sold me hither: for God did send me before you to preserve life.

Joseph let his brothers know it was God's Hand that had led him all along.

For these two years hath the famine been in the land: and yet there are five years, in the which there shall neither be earing nor harvest. And God sent me before you to preserve you a posterity in the earth, and to save your lives by a great deliverance.

Joseph recalled Pharaoh's dream nine years before, (Genesis 41:47, 54).

So now it was not you that sent me hither, but God: and He hath made me a father to Pharaoh, and lord of all his house, and a ruler throughout all the land of Egypt.

Haste ye, and go up to my father, and say unto him, Thus saith thy son Joseph, God hath made me lord of all Egypt: come down unto me, tarry not:

Joseph expressed his eagerness to see his own father.

and thou shalt dwell in the land of Goshen, and thou shalt be near unto me, thou, and thy children, and thy children's children, and thy flocks, and thy herds, and all that thou hast: and there will I nourish thee; for yet there are five years of famine; lest thou, and thy household, and all that thou hast, come to poverty.

Joseph promised to take care of his family for the rest of their lives.

And, behold, your eyes see, and the eyes of my brother Benjamin, that it is my mouth that speaketh unto you.

Joseph knew how unbelievable this was for them.

And ye shall tell my father of all my glory in Egypt, and of all that ye have seen; and ye shall haste and bring down my father hither. And he fell upon his brother Benjamin's neck, and wept; and Benjamin wept upon his neck. Moreover he kissed all his brethren, and wept upon them: and after that his brethren talked with him.

Joseph could finally be reunited with his birth family.

And the fame thereof was heard in Pharaoh's house, saying, Joseph's brethren are come: and it pleased Pharaoh well, and his servants.

The tremendous news brought joy to all who heard it.

And Pharaoh said unto Joseph, Say unto thy brethren, This do ye; lade your beasts, and go, get you unto the land of Canaan; and take your father and your households, and come unto me: and I will give you the good of the land of Egypt, and ye shall eat the fat of the land. Now thou art commanded, this do ye; take you wagons out of the land of Egypt for your little ones, and for your wives, and bring your father, and come. Also regard not your stuff; for the good of all the land of Egypt is yours.

Pharaoh was happy to provide for Joseph's family forever.

And the children of Israel did so: and Joseph gave them wagons, according to the commandment of Pharaoh, and gave them provision for the way. To all of them he gave each man changes of raiment; but to Benjamin he gave three hundred pieces of silver, and five changes of raiment. And to his father he sent after this manner; ten asses laden with the good things of Egypt, and ten she asses laden with corn and bread and meat for his father by the way.

They would impress to the utmost whomever met them.

So he sent his brethren away, and they departed: and he said unto them, See that ye fall not out by the way.

Joseph understood his brothers' excitement, and warned them not to lose focus of what was important.

And they went up out of Egypt, and came into the land of Canaan unto Jacob their father, and told him, saying, Joseph is yet alive, and he is governor of all the land of Egypt.

Jacob was not ready for this glorious news.

And Jacob's heart fainted, for he believed them not. And they told him all the words of Joseph, which he had said unto them: and when he saw the wagons which Joseph had sent to carry him, the spirit of Jacob their father revived:

God remembered His promise to Jacob, (Genesis 28:15).

and Israel said, It is enough; Joseph my son is yet alive: I will go and see him before I die.

Chapter 46

And Israel took his journey with all that he had, and came to Beersheba, and offered sacrifices unto the God of his father Isaac.

Jacob upheld his progenitors' covenant with God, and offered sacrifices in the same place his father Isaac had, (Genesis 26:25, 33).

And God spake unto Israel in the visions of the night, and said, Jacob, Jacob. And he said, Here am I. And He said, I am God, the God of thy father: fear not to go down into Egypt; for I will there make of thee a great nation: I will go down with thee into Egypt; and I will also surely bring thee up again: and Joseph shall put his hand upon thine eyes.

God was reassuring Jacob.

And Jacob rose up from Beersheba: and the sons of Israel carried Jacob their father, and their little ones, and their wives, in the wagons which Pharaoh had sent to carry him.

Jacob was now Egyptian aristocracy, and no longer needed to journey on foot.

And they took their cattle, and their goods, which they had gotten in the land of Canaan, and came into Egypt, Jacob, and all his seed with him: his sons, and his sons' sons with him, his daughters, and his sons' daughters, and all his seed brought he with him into Egypt.

Jacob's choice to obey God would result in the exceedingly abundant reproduction of his seed, (Exodus 1:7).

And these are the names of the children of Israel, which came into Egypt, Jacob and his sons: Rueben, Jacob's firstborn. And the sons of Rueben; Hanoch, and Phallu, and Hezron, and Carmi. And the sons of Simeon; Jemuel, and Jamin, and Ohad, and Jachin, and Zohar, and Shaul the son of a Canaanitish woman. And the sons of Levi; Gershon, Kohath, and Merari. And the sons of Judah; Er, and Onan, and Shelah, and Pharez, and Zerah: but Er and Onan died in the land of Canaan. And the sons of Pharez were Hezron and Hamul. And the sons of Issachar; Tola, and Phuvah, and Job, and Shimron. And the sons of Zebulun; Sered, and Elon, and Jahleel. These be the sons of Leah, which she bare unto Jacob in Padanaram, with his daughter Dinah: all the souls of his sons and his daughters were thirty and three. And the sons of Gad; Ziphion, and Haggi, Shuni, and Ezbon, Eri, and Arodi, and Areli. And the sons of Asher; Jimnah, and Ishuah, and Isui, and Beriah, and Serah their sister: and the sons of Beriah; Heber, and Malchiel. These are the sons of Zilpah, whom Laban gave to Leah his daughter, and these she bare unto

Jacob, even sixteen souls. The sons of Rachel Jacob's wife; Joseph, and Benjamin. And unto Joseph in the land of Egypt were born Manasseh and Ephraim, which Asenath the daughter of Potipherah priest of On bare unto him. And the sons of Benjamin were Belah, and Becher, and Ashbel, Gera, and Naaman, Ehi, and Rosh, Muppim, and Huppim, and Ard. These are the sons of Rachel, which were born to Jacob: all the souls were fourteen. And the sons of Dan; Hushim. And the sons of Naphtali; Jahzeel, and Guni, and Jezer, and Shillem. These are the sons of Bilhah, which Laban gave unto Rachel his daughter, and she bare these unto Jacob: all the souls were seven. All the souls that came with Jacob into Egypt, which came out of his loins, besides Jacob's sons' wives, all the souls were threescore and six; and the sons of Joseph, which were born him in Egypt, were two souls: all the souls of the house of Jacob, which came into Egypt, were threescore and ten.

From these seventy people would descend the entire nation of Israel, (Numbers 1:20-43, 47).

And he sent Judah before him unto Joseph, to direct his face unto Goshen; and they came into the land of Goshen.

Judah continued to exhibit leadership.

And Joseph made ready his chariot, and went up to meet Israel his father, to Goshen, and presented himself unto him; and he fell on his neck, and wept on his neck a good while.

Joseph had not seen his father in twenty-two years.

And Israel said unto Joseph, Now let me die, since I have seen thy face, because thou art yet alive.

Israel was content with having been reunited with his son.

And Joseph said unto his brethren, and unto his father's house, I will go up, and shew Pharaoh, and say unto him, My brethren, and my father's house, which were in the land of Canaan, are come unto me; and the men are shepherds, for their trade hath been to feed cattle; and they have brought their flocks, and their herds, and all that they have. And it shall come to pass, when Pharaoh shall call you, and shall say, What is your occupation? That ye shall say, Thy servants' trade hath been about cattle from our youth even until now, both we, and also our fathers: that ye may dwell in the land of Goshen; for every shepherd is an abomination unto the Egyptians.

Joseph took advantage of his knowledge of Egyptian society to benefit his brothers.

Chapter 47

Then Joseph came and told Pharaoh, and said, My father and my brethren, and their flocks, and their herds, and all that they have, are come out of the land of Canaan; and, behold, they are in the land of Goshen. And he took some of his brethren, even five men, and presented them unto Pharaoh.

Joseph proudly introduced five of his brothers to Pharaoh.

And Pharaoh said unto his brethren, What is your occupation? And they said unto Pharaoh, Thy servants are shepherds, both we, and also our fathers. They said moreover unto Pharaoh, For to sojourn in the land are we come; for thy servants have no pasture for their flocks; for the famine is sore in the land of Canaan: now therefore, we pray thee, let thy servants dwell in the land of Goshen.

Joseph's brothers were careful to follow Joseph's instructions.

And Pharaoh spake unto Joseph, saying, Thy father and thy brethren are come unto thee: the land of Egypt is before thee; in the best of the land make thy father and brethren to dwell; in the land of Goshen let them dwell: and if thou knowest any men of activity among them, then make them rulers over my cattle.

Pharaoh believed his nation would be further blessed by the arrival of Joseph's family.

And Joseph brought in Jacob his father, and set him before Pharaoh: and Jacob blessed Pharaoh. And Pharaoh said unto Jacob, How old art thou?

Pharaoh was filled with awe and admiration upon meeting this esteemed patriarch.

And Jacob said unto Pharaoh, The days of the years of my pilgrimage are an hundred and thirty years: few and evil have the days of the years of my life been, and have not attained unto the days of the years of the life of my fathers in the days of their pilgrimage.

Jacob would neither outlive his father, (Genesis 35:28), nor his grandfather, (Genesis 25:7).

And Jacob blessed Pharaoh, and went out from before Pharaoh.

These men were mutually privileged to have been in each other's presence.

And Joseph placed his father and his brethren, and gave them a possession in the land of Egypt, in the best of the land, in the land of Rameses, as Pharaoh had commanded.

Joseph wanted his family to prosper.

And Joseph nourished his father, and his brethren, and all his father's household, with bread, according to their families. And there was no bread in all the land; for the famine was very sore, so that the land of Egypt and all the land of Canaan fainted by reason of the famine.

Jacob and his family were safe in Goshen.

And Joseph gathered up all the money that was found in the land of Egypt, and in the land of Canaan, for the corn which they bought: and Joseph brought the money into Pharaoh's house.

Pharaoh became one of the richest men on Earth.

And when money failed in the land of Egypt, and in the land of Canaan, all the Egyptians came unto Joseph, and said, Give us bread: for why should we die in thy presence? For the money faileth.

The famine was catastrophic, and lasted until the economy of the entire area was devastated.

And Joseph said, Give your cattle; and I will give you for your cattle, if money fail.

Joseph had compassion on the helpless victims.

And they brought their cattle unto Joseph: and Joseph gave them bread in exchange for horses, and for the flocks, and for the cattle of the herds, and for the asses: and he fed them with bread for all their cattle for that year.

They now had no commodities left to trade for food.

When that year was ended, they came unto him the second year, and said unto him, We will not hide it from my lord, how that our money is spent; my lord also hath our herds of cattle; there is not ought left in the sight of my lord, but our bodies, and our lands: wherefore shall we die before thine eyes, both we and our land? Buy us and our land for bread, and we and our land will be servants unto Pharaoh: and give us seed, that we may live, and not die, that the land be not desolate.

Pharaoh's subjects earnestly pleaded with Joseph to give them food.

And Joseph bought all the land of Egypt for Pharaoh; for the Egyptians sold every man his field, because the famine prevailed over them: so the land became Pharaoh's. And as for the people, he removed them to cities from one end of the borders of Egypt even to the other end thereof. Only the land of the priests bought he not; for the priests had a portion assigned them of Pharaoh, and did eat their portion which Pharaoh gave them: wherefore they sold not their lands.

They were now of lower status than the Hebrews.

Then Joseph said unto the people, Behold, I have bought you this day and your land for Pharaoh: lo, here is seed for you, and ye shall sow the land. And it shall come to pass in the increase, that ye shall give the fifth part unto Pharaoh, and

four parts shall be your own, for seed of the field, and for your food, and for them of your households, and for food for your little ones.

Joseph proposed a plan that would sustain them.

And they said, Thou hast saved our lives: let us find grace in the sight of my lord, and we will be Pharaoh's servants.

They were thankful to Joseph for having spared their lives.

And Joseph made it a law over the land of Egypt unto this day, that Pharaoh should have the fifth part; except the land of the priests only, which became not Pharaoh's.

Hebrew dominance in Egypt would last until their slavery, (Exodus 1:11).

And Israel dwelt in the land of Egypt, in the country of Goshen; and they had possessions therein, and grew, and multiplied exceedingly.

God remembered His promise to Jacob, (Genesis 46:3).

And Jacob lived in the land of Egypt seventeen years: so the whole age of Jacob was an hundred forty and seven years. And the time drew nigh that Israel must die: and he called his son Joseph, and said unto him, If now I have found grace in thy sight, put, I pray thee, thy hand under my thigh, and deal kindly and truly with me; bury me not, I pray thee, in Egypt: but I will lie with my fathers, and thou shalt carry me out of Egypt, and bury me in their burying place.

Jacob believed in God's promises, (Genesis 46:4, Genesis 15:14).

And he said, I will do as thou hast said. And he said, Swear unto me. And he sware unto him.

Joseph wanted to do what he could for his dying father.

And Israel bowed himself upon the bed's head.

Israel was relieved to know that he would once again reach the Promised Land.

Chapter 48

And it came to pass after these things, that one told Joseph, Behold, thy father is sick: and he took with him his two sons, Manasseh and Ephraim. And one told Jacob, and said, Behold, thy son Joseph cometh unto thee: and Israel strengthened himself, and sat upon the bed.

Jacob used his last remaining strength to bestow a parting blessing on his grandsons.

And Jacob said unto Joseph, God Almighty appeared unto me at Luz in the land of Canaan, and blessed me, and said unto me, Behold, I will make thee fruitful, and multiply thee, and I will make of thee a multitude of people; and will give this land to thy seed after thee for an everlasting possession. And now thy two sons, Ephraim and Manasseh, which were born unto thee in the land of Egypt before I came unto thee into Egypt, are mine; as Rueben and Simeon, they shall be mine.

The blessing intended for Rueben and Simeon, Jacob's first two sons, would be given instead to Ephraim and Manasseh, Joseph's two sons.

And thy issue, which thou begettest after them, shall be thine, and shall be called after the name of their brethren in their inheritance.

In this way Joseph would be repaid for everything he had been through.

And as for me, when I came from Padan, Rachel died be me in the land of Canaan in the way, when yet there was but a little way to come unto Ephrath: and I buried her there in the way of Ephrath; the same is Bethlehem.

Jacob prophesied, letting Joseph know the place where his Hope would come from, (Micah 5:2).

And Israel beheld Joseph's sons, and said, Who are these?

Jacob was growing more and more unaware of his surroundings.

And Joseph said unto his father, They are my sons, whom God hath given me in this place. And he said, Bring them, I pray thee, unto me, and I will bless them.

Jacob desired to pass down the birthright blessing given to him by Isaac.

Now the eyes of Israel were dim for age, so that he could not see. And he brought them near unto him; and he kissed them, and embraced them. And Israel said unto Joseph, I had not thought to see thy face: and, lo, God hath shewed me also thy seed.

Jacob expressed his thankfulness to God for having brought his son back to him.

And Joseph brought them out from between his knees, and he bowed himself with his face to the earth. And Joseph took them both, Ephraim in his right hand toward Israel's left hand, and Manasseh in his left hand toward Israel's right hand, and brought them near unto him.

Joseph expected the birthright blessing to be passed down to his eldest son, Manasseh.

And Israel stretched out his right hand, and laid it upon Ephraim's head, who was the younger, and his left hand upon Manasseh's head, guiding his hands wittingly; for Manasseh was the firstborn.

Jacob purposefully bestowed it upon Ephraim, Joseph's younger son.

And he blessed Joseph, and said, God, before whom my fathers Abraham and Isaac did walk, the God which fed me all my life long unto this day, the Angel which redeemed me from all evil, bless the lads; and let my name be named on them, and the name of my fathers Abraham and Isaac; and let them grow into a multitude in the midst of the earth.

Jacob was proud of the offspring of Joseph.

And when Joseph saw that his father laid his right hand upon the head of Ephraim, it displeased him:

Joseph was worried that his father's poor eyesight had caused him to err.

and he held up his father's hand, to remove it from Ephraim's head unto Manasseh's head.

He sought to rectify his father's mistake.

And Joseph said unto his father, Not so, my father: for this is the firstborn; put thy right hand upon his head. And his father refused, and said, I know it, my son,

I know it: he also shall become a people, and he also shall be great: but truly his younger brother shall be greater than he, and his seed shall become a multitude of nations.

Jacob had witnessed the younger brother inherit the birthright in place of the older brother on multiple occasions, and knew that God had a way of bringing about the unexpected.

And he blessed them that day, saying, In thee shall Israel bless, saying, God make thee as Ephraim and as Manasseh: and he set Ephraim before Manasseh.

He solidified the blessing.

And Israel said unto Joseph, Behold, I die: but God shall be with you, and bring you again unto the land of your fathers. Moreover I have given to thee one portion above thy brethren, which I took out of the hand of the Amorite with my sword and with my bow.

Jacob continued to show favor to Rachel's firstborn.

Chapter 49

And Jacob called unto his sons, and said, Gather yourselves together, that I may tell you that which shall befall you in the last days. Gather yourselves together, and hear, ye sons of Jacob; and hearken unto Israel your father.

Jacob gave each of his twelve sons foresight into the future.

Reuben, thou art my firstborn, my might, and the beginning of my strength, the excellency of dignity, and the excellency of power: unstable as water, thou shalt not excel; because thou wentest up to thy father's bed; then defiledst thou it: he went up to my couch.

Reuben's treacherous act had not been forgotten by Jacob.

Simeon and Levi are brethren; instruments of cruelty are in their habitations. O my soul, come not thou into their secret; unto their assembly, mine honor, be not thou united: for in their anger they slew a man, and in their selfwill they digged down a wall. Cursed be their anger, for it was fierce; and their wrath, for it was cruel: I will divide them in Jacob, and scatter them in Israel.

Jacob's displeasure with these two sons resulted in their permanent loss of inheritance in Israel, (Numbers 1:47, Joshua 19:9).

Judah, thou art he whom thy brethren shall praise: thy hand shall be in the neck of thine enemies; thy father's children shall bow down before thee. Judah is a lion's whelp: from the prey, my son, thou art gone up: he stooped down, he couched as a lion, and as an old lion; who shall rouse him up? The scepter shall not depart from Judah, nor a lawgiver from between his feet, until Shiloh come; and unto him shall the gathering of the people be. His eyes shall be red with wine, and his teeth white with milk.

Jacob had hope in Judah's Seed, (Matthew 1:2-16).

Zebulun shall dwell at the haven of the sea; and he shall be for an haven of ships; and his border shall be unto Zidon.

Zebulun would be at peace with his Canaanite neighbors.

Issachar is a strong ass couching down between two burdens: and he saw that rest was good, and the land that it was pleasant; and bowed his shoulder to bear, and became a servant unto tribute.

Issachar was given the characteristic of a donkey, and would one day be the proud forefather of Barak, a prince who would one day help deliver Israel from their Canaanite oppressors, (Judges 5:15).

Dan shall judge his people, as one of the tribes of Israel. Dan shall be a serpent by the way, an adder in the path, that biteth the horse heels, so that his rider shall fall backward.

A Hebrew word for "judge", Dan would one day be the proud forefather of the man who led out in designing Solomon's temple, (2 Chronicles 2:14).

I have waited for thy salvation, O LORD.

Jacob could hardly contain his excitement.

Gad, a troop shall overcome him: but he shall overcome at the last.

This tribe would one day help their fellow Israelites conquer the land of Canaan, (Numbers 32:1-32).

Out of Asher his bread shall be fat, and he shall yield royal dainties.

A descendant of this tribe would one day provide food for king Solomon's household, (1 Kings 4:7-16).

Naphtali is a hind let loose: he giveth goodly words.

It was in the region of this tribe that the Messiah would one day spread His message of hope, (Matthew 4:13-17).

Joseph is a fruitful bough, even a fruitful bough by a well; whose branches run over the wall: the archers have sorely grieved him, and shot at him, and hated him: but his bow abode in strength, and the arms of his hands were made strong by the hands of the mighty God of Jacob; (from thence is the shepherd, the stone of Israel): even by the God of thy father, who shall help thee; and by the Almighty, who shall bless thee with blessings of heaven above, blessings of the deep that lieth under, blessings of the breasts, and of the womb: the blessings of thy father have prevailed above the blessings of my progenitors unto the utmost bound of the everlasting hills: they shall be on the head of Joseph, and on the crown of the head of him that was separate from his brethren.

The most elaborate blessing was reserved for Jacob's favorite son.

Benjamin shall ravin as a wolf: in the morning he shall devour the prey, and at night he shall divide the spoil.

This tribe would produce some of Israel's fiercest warriors, (1 Chronicles 12:2).

All these are the twelve tribes of Israel: and this is it that their father spake unto them, and blessed them; every one according to his blessing he blessed them. And he charged them, and said unto them, I am to be gathered unto my people: bury me with my fathers in the cave that is in the field of Ephron the Hittite, in the cave that is in the field of Machpelah, which is before Mamre, in the land of Canaan, which Abraham bought with the field of Ephron the Hittite

for a possession of a burying place. There they buried Abraham and Sarah his wife; there they buried Isaac and Rebekah his wife; and there I buried Leah. The purchase of the field and of the cave that is therein was from the children of Heth.

Jacob wanted to be buried next to Leah, the wife whom he had originally not favored, (Genesis 29:30).

And when Jacob had made an end of commanding his sons, he gathered up his feet into the bed, and yielded up the ghost, and was gathered unto his people.

Thus ended the story of Israel, the prince of God, (Genesis 32:28).

Chapter 50

And Joseph fell upon his father's face, and wept upon him, and kissed him. And Joseph commanded his servants the physicians to embalm his father: and the physicians embalmed Israel. And forty days were fulfilled for him; for so are fulfilled the days of those which are embalmed: and the Egyptians mourned for him threescore and ten days.

Joseph's grief was intense, as was his Egyptian observers'.

And when the days of his mourning were past, Joseph spake unto the house of Pharaoh, saying, If now I have found grace in your eyes, speak, I pray you, in the ears of Pharaoh, saying, My father made me swear, saying, Lo, I die: in my grave which I have digged for me in the land of Canaan, there shalt thou bury me. Now therefore let me go up, I pray thee, and bury my father, and I will come again.

Joseph remembered his promise to his father, (Genesis 47:29-31).

And Pharaoh said, Go up, and bury thy father, according as he made thee swear.

Pharaoh honored his servant's request.

And Joseph went up to bury his father: and with him went up all the servants of Pharaoh, the elders of his house, and all the elders of the land of Egypt, and all the house of Joseph, and his brethren, and his father's house: only their little ones, and their flocks, and their herds, they left in the land of Goshen. And there went up with him both chariots and horsemen: and it was a very great company.

The next Pharaoh would not be so lenient, (Exodus 1:8, Exodus 5:1, 2).

And they came to the threshing floor of Atad, which is beyond Jordan, and there they mourned with a great and very sore lamentation: and he made a mourning for his father seven days. And when the inhabitants of the land, the Canaanites, saw the mourning in the floor of Atad, they said, This is a grievous mourning to the Egyptians: wherefore the name of it was called Abelmizraim, which is beyond Jordan.

The Canaanites memorialized the place of mourning with a permanent expression of the Egyptians' sadness.

And his sons did unto him as he commanded them: for his sons carried him into the land of Canaan, and buried him in the cave of the field of Machpelah, which Abraham bought with the field for a possession of a burying place of Ephron the Hittite, before Mamre.

Their kind act towards their father would be rewarded, (Genesis 50:21).

And Joseph returned into Egypt, he, and his brethren, and all that went up with him to bury his father, after he had buried his father. And when Joseph's brethren saw that their father was dead, they said, Joseph will peradventure hate us, and will certainly requite us all the evil which we did unto him. And they sent a messenger unto Joseph, saying, Thy father did command before he died, saying, So shall ye say unto Joseph, Forgive, I pray thee now, the trespass of thy brethren, and their sin; for they did unto thee evil: and now, we pray thee, forgive the trespass of the servants of the God of thy father.

Joseph's brothers did not believe they could survive his retaliation.

And Joseph wept when they spake unto him.

Joseph pitied them.

And his brethren also went and fell down before his face; and they said, Behold, we be thy servants. And Joseph said unto them, Fear not: for am I in the place of God? But as for you, ye thought evil against me; but God meant it unto good, to bring to pass, as it is this day, to save much people alive. Now therefore fear ye not: I will nourish you, and your little ones. And he comforted them, and spake kindly unto them.

Joseph's promise to them would last as long as he lived.

And Joseph dwelt in Egypt, he, and his father's house: and Joseph lived an hundred and ten years. And Joseph saw Ephraim's children of the third generation: the children also of Machir the son of Manasseh were brought up upon Joseph's knees.

Sirak James

Joseph lived a long, full life.

And Joseph said unto his brethren, I die: and God will surely visit you, and bring you out of this land unto the land which he sware to Abraham, to Isaac, and to Jacob. And Joseph took an oath of the children of Israel, saying, God will surely visit you, and ye shall carry up my bones from hence.

The children of Israel would not forget their promise to Joseph, (Exodus 13:19).

So Joseph died, being an hundred and ten years old: and they embalmed him, and he was put in a coffin in Egypt.

Thus ends the story of Joseph, and so begins the story of the Exodus, (Exodus)!

About the Author

Sirak James was born in Addis Ababa, Ethiopia. He graduated from Union College in Lincoln, Nebraska, with a BA in piano pedagogy, and is currently a member of the Atlanta Metro Seventh-Day Adventist Church.

Printed in the United States
By Bookmasters